Abandoned Before Birth/ United in Prison

A Father & His Biological Son

Living Together as Cellmates

Abandoned Before Birth/ United in Prison

A Father & His Biological Son

Living Together as Cellmates

Paul D. Scott Sr. &

Co-Author: Paul D. Scott Jr.

Heads Up Publications

Atlanta

Abandoned before Birth/ United in Prison
Subtitle: A Father & His Biological Son.
Living Together as Cellmates
Copyright © 2020 by Paul D. Scott Sr. & Co – Author Paul D. Scott Jr.
Published by Heads Up Publications
Cover by Pierre McCummings

ISBN: 978-1-7346026-2-3
Ebook ISBN: 978-1-7346026-3-0
Library of Congress Control Number: 2020905586

Heads Up Publications Books are available at special discounts for bulk purchases for sales or premiums.
Direct all inquiries and correspondence to:
Heads Up Publications
P.O Box 162593
Atlanta, GA 30321
e-mail/ headsuppublications@gmail.com

Printed in the United States of America

In Memory of:

My Mother, Nonie Bowen Scott
My Father, Bonnie Scott Sr.
My Grandmother, Lila Miles Bowen
My Sister, Pamela Scott Barnes
Cynthia Moore
Rose Moore
Kenny Moore Sr.
Reggie Moore

This Book is Dedicated to:

All the parents and children who have not been able to share a relationship with each other. And, especially dedicated to any parents who were in custody or any other situation which prevented them from being present in their child/children lives when they were born.

Most importantly, this book it dedicated to all the children who have never met their biological mother and or father and desire to do so who struggle with abandonment issues.

Contents

Introduction

Abandoned before Birth/United in Prison *Subtitle*: A Father & His Biological Son Living Together as Cellmates. This book is based on a true story. About a father and son's relationship. How our first chance of living together was in a prison cell.

Lil Paul felt the pain of abandonment from his father for many years before he had a chance to express his emotions. Consequently, many walls of distrust, frustration, anger, doubt, blame, shame, guilt, isolation and hurt took form in Lil Paul's development. And, truth be told, still being addressed to this very day, although, much healing has taken place for us both. However, it was a difficult journey for us to get there. What we had to endure to stay cellmates for four years in the same prison without getting separated is unbelievable and unheard of.

However, we managed to accomplish this task and survived to share with the world how we did it. I was serving a life sentence and my son seven years. We both are home now living successful Godly lives. But we went through much pain, suffering, temptation and persecution to get here. At some point, divine intervention took place or it was there all along; either way, you will draw your own conclusion after you finish reading a book which is intended to save lives, bring families back together, heal deep wounds, address issues of abandonment, rejection and betrayal.

Foreword

PAUL D. SCOTT SR. has innate leadership skills. It was fortunate for me he chose to use those skills for the benefit of our Chapel Ministry at the California Men's Colony State Prison. The inmate population and staff at the prison experienced Paul's daily influence, which improved the behavior of those with whom he served. My privilege was being Paul's supervisor, as his gifts for working with varied personalities were put into action. This was a career godsend for me. If Paul Scott made a statement, we could go to the bank with it. I expect this book's impact to be signature PAUL D. SCOTT SR.

– Rev. H. Warren Alderson
Protestant Chaplain California Men's Colony | 1988 – 2018

Chapter 1

Encounters of Prison Visitations

L il Paul's mother brought him to see me for the first time when he was 18 months old. I was at the California Men's Colony, located in San Luis Obispo, California. Please keep this Institution in mind. It will play a role of great significance in later chapters. Prior to this occasion, I had only received photographs of my son. I had always imagined how it would feel the first time I had a chance to hold my son in my arms. Here it was, 18 months following the day, June 25, 1981, when I talked with his mother over the phone and she informed me that he had been born. I held him close to my heart, asked his mother to excuse us for a moment and I took a walk over to the children's play area. Yes, this was our first opportunity to bond at any capacity. So, instinctively I did what I thought would leave a strong impression upon his mind. We played around for several minutes before returning to the company of his mother. I was greatly appreciative of this experience. There was no resistance whatsoever. It was as if he innately knew exactly who I was. That caused me to feel joy and very grateful to his mother for preserving his identity and protecting the Scott trait. I was surprised by the fact that his mother knew more about me than I thought she did. I discovered she was transmitting parts of my character to him, which I had no idea she had done or was willing to do.

Sherry, Lil Paul's mother, was aware of Victoria, my wife, but Sherry did not hold me not marrying her against my son by not allowing him to see me. Although Sherry did have many questions for me. There was lots of explaining I had to do. Sherry wanted answers and I did my best, to be honest in my answers she accepted what I presented for the time being. But, she was not completely satisfied with my explanation and advised me that she was going to need further clarification to be at peace. I assured Sherry that her request would be granted. However, I motioned for us to spend the remainder of the visit, including Lil Paul, in on the interactions since he was the center of attention. She agreed and we allowed the few moments which remained in visiting to be spent focused on Lil Paul.

This was Sherry's first time witnessing Lil Paul and me becoming acquainted. She seemed to be enjoying his and my bonding just as much, if not more, as we did. The expression on her face told it all. For a split second, I felt a form of freedom like never before. I was taken back to the last time Sherry and I were together in society, which was the actual occasion Lil Paul was conceived. I began to stare into space. Sherry asked me "what was wrong?" A cold chill came over my body and I jumped to my feet, simultaneously shaking it off and answering her question, "nothing!" I had no comprehension of what was transpiring this very moment other than it being something beyond human understanding. What I do know is that this was the first time I saw my son in person. And it had a very profound effect on me.

Visiting was concluding. Lil Paul was asleep. Sherry woke him up. We embraced, said our goodbyes and went in our appropriate directions. It is customary with most prisoners, when returning from visiting with family or friends, to be left alone. Convicts prefer returning to their cell and kicking back, letting the full effects of their visit settle. It is one way of holding on to those precious moments as long as possible that were just shared with people you hold close to your heart. I reclined on my bunk and reminisced. I remembered some of the conversations Lil Paul's mother and I would have. The last time we were together, we discussed how our children would be raised if we ever had any together. The amazing thing is she got pregnant on this occasion, which was two days before my arrest. We had been involved for close to 2 years. However, she didn't conceive until the last time we were together in society, September 29, 1980. Please keep the month September in mind because it was not only the month my son was conceived; it also is the month my grandson was born 17 years later. The phenomenal thing about it, my grandson's birthday is on the exact same date that Victoria and I spent together in society, September 24th.

Sherry and I didn't get married because of the commitment Victoria and I had made prior to my arrest. Victoria was my High School sweetheart. She had a scholarship at San Diego State University and was enrolled for her first semester when I was arrested. I drove her to San Diego from Pasadena, California and stayed with her that first week of college. September 23, 1980, was the last day we spent having fun together. We went sightseeing and experienced recreation and entertainment like never before. We discussed marriage, my moving to San Diego and us starting a family. Early the morning of September 24, 1980, I said goodbye to Victoria as I was heading back to Pasadena. It was goodbye for sure as far as my freedom was concerned. Although I had planned to return in a week after I made some money, that week came and past because seven days later on, October 1, 1980, I was arrested and placed in custody.

Victoria and I did manage to maintain a relationship while I was in the Los Angeles County Jail. She even moved back to

Pasadena, California, after her first semester ended at San Diego State. She sacrificed a four-year scholarship as a result of the devastation she experienced from my arrest. She did, however, continue with her education by enrolling in Pasadena City College. She worked a job on the side for pocket money, which provided her the finances to come to visit me regularly. Yes, Victoria was aware of the past that Sherry and I had. But, she had no idea she was pregnant. Victoria had already moved back to Pasadena when she did find out.

The discovery was not pretty. Victoria wanted to know if Sherry was pregnant by me. I confessed to my transgression and admitted the child could very well be mine. She was very angry and disappointed with me. I did apologize and asked for forgiveness. I let Victoria know how important she was to me and how much I needed her in my life. But that if this were something she couldn't recover from, I would understand and accept her decision. Victoria wanted time to think about whether she wanted to continue our relationship or not. She evaluated our relationship, weighed the commitment and debated with many emotions. Love rose supreme and Victoria chose to stay with me.

Victoria was faithful throughout the court procedures and even came and testified on my behalf, which proved I wasn't such a bad guy after all. She was terribly disappointed by the verdict. However, she held herself together. She agreed to proceed with the marriage commitment we had discussed before my arrest and while in custody, even if I was found guilty. And, once I got to the facility

which afforded us the opportunity, we would get married. On
January 22, 1982, at the California Men's Colony, we did get
married.

I had communicated with Sherry consistently via mail and
institution permitted phone calls. She sent me weekly photos of Lil
Paul, which allowed me to be as much part of his development as
possible. Although we had some pleasant communication, Sherry
had a way of letting me know that I was not entirely off the hook.
She reminded me on a regular basis that I still had some explaining
to do. I promised to make an entire disclosure when she came to visit
me again. We agreed to a date that would be convenient for us both
and the deal was sealed.

"Paul Scott, report to control corridor for a visit," was the
announcement over the Institution paging system. It was Sherry and
my son. She kept her word was all I could think. I was overjoyed
with excitement. Aside from what I needed to discuss with Sherry
about my marrying Victoria, this was the second time I would be
seeing my son in person. That alone meant more to me than I was
able to express. I was just sincerely gratefully and tried to display it
the best I could. We greeted in the normal and permitted fashion.
Without delay, I went into my act. At this juncture in my
confinement, I had only been in for three years. Therefore, I had not
developed into the profound intellectual giant most convicted felons
do who manage to talk their way out of anything. But, my mind was
made up; that I was faced with the fight of my life and had to win. I
had to win Sherry over by convincing her somehow to seeing things

my way. It was obvious; she had her guard up at first. The expression on her face was not one of her own. Evidently, someone had been in her ear. It resembled a welcoming, but the wall was up and there was a firm distance. Nevertheless, I had to go to work and after about 15 minutes into my explaining, she began, to loosen up and became more relaxed. In fact, she started asking questions with a form of concern and emotion attached. This helped me relax a little and boosted my confidence. But, I did not take that for granted. My main concern was to make sure nothing interfered with me having a relationship with my son. Sherry promised never to allow my son to be punished for my decisions. Furthermore, she agreed to never allow anyone or anything to interfere with my son and my relationship. This agreement even included Victoria! Sherry gave approval for Victoria to bring my son on visits with the stipulation that another family member of mine was able to attend. Victoria was pleased with this arrangement and had no problem with Sherry bringing Lil Paul to visit his father just as long as it didn't collide with her scheduled visits. In fact, Victoria would hint around and say, "you can't do any more damage than you already have!"

Visiting was reaching the hour of termination. I made certain Lil Paul and I had our intervals for quality time. Sherry focused her entire attention on our every move. It was as if she was absorbing as much of my personality as she could. I perceived it as her, including herself, in on Lil Paul and my interaction. Years later, I found out she was ingesting the features she admired about me the most so that she could instill them in Lil Paul in my absence. Our visit was great and I felt an abundance of pressure relieved. We concluded with a proper understanding, at lease that what impression I was under. Sherry advised me as we said our goodbyes that she didn't know when she would be able to bring Lil Paul to revisit me because of her financial status. I was totally blindsided by that and it shook me up something terrible. I couldn't even reply because the visiting doors were closing. I thought to myself, "damn, she should have told me that at the beginning of the visit, not the end." "You picked a fine time to leave me, Lucille!"

Sherry didn't bring Lil Paul to visit me again until September 24, 1988, although she did maintain a constant line of communication with me via mail and telephone conversations. I talked with Lil Paul over the phone twice a month. My family, mother, father, sisters, brothers, nieces and nephews, brought Lil Paul to visit me quite frequently. Even my homeboy, E.B., brought Lil Paul and my mother to visit me twice me a couple of times. I had another homeboy, Kevin DeJohnette, who was my best friend, bring my mother to visit me once. I included that piece to primarily point out the fact that Kevin's son and Lil Paul became best friends in High School without even knowing that their fathers knew each other. Furthermore, Kevin's son is my grandson's godfather. Was all this predestined?

Chapter 2

Disappointment & Devastation

The date was coming up for my sixth appearance before the Board of Prison Terms for parole consideration hearing. I had done everything humanly possible to be found suitable for release. I had endured the most severe forms of trauma that are known for sending the average person over the edge and I managed to maintain my stability as well as sanity. I had lost my father to cancer, grandmother, the only grandparent I knew, to old age and my oldest sister to an overdose of drugs. I was not permitted to attend any of their funerals. My mother was confined to a bed in a convalescent home, following a massive stroke and was not expected to recover. "My God, how much more do I have to endure, Lord, before the gates are opened?" This was the periodic question I would ask God when my heart was heavy.

My 20th year of incarceration was closing in and I had been blessed considering the environment(s) I had been in. Most of my days were fairly decent, provided I stayed in the moment. Taking advantage of every activity in which I could associate with being equivalent to something productive in society was my philosophy and constitution. Most important, though, was the faith that I profess and the relationship I had with my Lord and Savior Jesus Christ. I was allowed to make weekly phone calls. I had received a letter from Lil Paul's mother asking me to call her as soon as possible because there was something very important, she needed to tell me. It had been a while since Sherry and I last talked. So, I got around to making the call. However, I didn't make it soon enough.

One evening after dinner, I was hanging out on the prison yard having a conversation with some fellow prisoners. A Muslim friend of mine named Hafiz politely approached the group of us, greeted everyone and asked if he could have a word with me. I acknowledged and excused myself from the group. Hafiz informed me that he had just gotten off the phone from talking with John T. and was told that my son was in the Los Angeles County Jail fighting attempt of murder chargers. Now, I knew Hafiz from the streets before even coming to prison. In fact, I knew who John T. was as well because we were in the life, drug game, at one time. John T.'s son and Lil Paul grew up together and ran the streets. So, I instantly could understand how this was coming in. I thanked Hafiz for the heads up on my son and I dismissed myself for the evening from the gathering. I knew what was so important for Sherry to tell me now. Anger hit me and I was not thinking clearly. My mind began to race and blame everybody. I had not even gotten any of the facts yet. I was off the hook with blaming people and had to catch myself. I took some deep breathes and calmed my mind down. I asked God to forgive me for overreacting and to make a way for me to get the facts.

So, I phoned Sherry! She confirmed everything Hafiz had shared with me. I didn't let Sherry know that I had already gotten word. She was very worried and terribly upset. Sherry was concerned that what happened to me was going to happen to Lil Paul. There was a gun involved in the incident. California's law in 2000-2001 was 10-20-life, use a gun go to prison. Plus, the District Attorney's office was trying to attach gang activities, which would have enhanced the charges. I was able to put my feelings to the side and console Sherry the best I could. She wanted to come to visit me the following Saturday and go more into the details surrounding Lil Paul's overall situation. I assured her that it would be perfectly fine with me and, especially since Victoria and I had been divorced. I did have Sherry provide me with Lil Paul's booking number and the Los

Angeles County Jail address. She pleaded with me not to write to him until she had a chance to visit me. I couldn't understand why this was such an issue, but I agreed. Our phone call ended, but the conversation didn't; at least in my mind.

I was infuriated. I was walking the track, talking to myself, trying to figure out what in the heck was happening. This was not my normal demeanor. As I made a couple of laps, a few guys who knew my style checked in with me. "Hey, hey brother Paul, what's cooking, you good?" "All is well, I'm just processing some news from home," was my reply. I continued my walking, having a conversation with myself. Although, in my head, I was conversing with several different people, giving them a piece of my mind. I was angry and the majority of it was toward myself, I just didn't know it. The question I kept asking myself, "could I have done anything different that would have prevented Lil Paul from being in Jail?"

It had been three years since I last saw Lil Paul. He was 16 years old then. He came up with my sister Ann, niece Sonya and her two children Jazmine and Lil Tim. All the signs were evident then that he was associated with some kind of gang affiliation. He was 13 years old when I first saw the gang banging features in him. We were on a visit at Chuckawalla Valley State Prison in Blythe, California. My mother and Brother Vic had brought him to see me. I asked Lil Paul then if he was involved in any gang activities and he said yes. I pulled him to the side and begun to come down on him pretty hard. My mother noticed and she immediately got my attention. Her exact words to me were, "look, Lil Paul doesn't need you to tell him what he is doing is wrong. He knows it's wrong! He needs you to love him and show him that you miss him and care about him. Now, you stop all that other stuff." Nina from Pasadena, the matriarch, had spoken. Out of respect and honor for my mother, there was an instant submission and cooperation. Lil Paul even noticed that whatever granny had said to me that it changed my demeanor. For the sake of clarification, my initial intentions were caring but the way I was presenting it did not come across in a caring manner, which caused Lil Paul to be on the defensive rather than receptive. Later during the visit, my mother was able to explain to me that the visiting room was not a place to straighten people out. Instead, it was a place to work things out. She thanked me for following her advice and went on to state, "Paul, I was not trying to take away your right to exercise your authority as a father when I addressed you. Your son really loves you and he is having it hard enough on him with you being in here. You have to love him before you can discipline him. Otherwise, you add to his wounds and may not get a chance to repair the damage especially, in these prison visiting rooms, because the visiting hours are too short." I truly thanked my mother for her advice. Lil Paul and my brother Vic had just returned to the table from the vending machines.

The most meaningful visit I recall being on with Lil Paul, aside from when he was small and his mother and Victoria brought him, was when he was 10 years old. I was in San Quentin. My mother brought him on a Family Visit. A Family Visit is when an inmate is allowed to be with his immediate family for a couple of days inside a trailer. The family is able to bring food from home and cook just as if they were in their own kitchen. There was even a basketball court for the family visitors at San Quentin. I had participated in the Family Visiting program at two other institutions. San Quentin was the only one that had a basketball court. Lil Paul and I had our first experience of any real athletic recreation together. We played a couple of games and I won. We went and ate a little lunch and went back out to play some more. Lil Paul eventually won. He couldn't run fast enough to go tell granny that he beat his dad playing basketball. Granny wasn't buying it and told him your daddy let you win. So, Lil Paul had to return and ask me if I let him win? My answer was, "no son, you won that on your own." Oh, he was just full of joy and couldn't wait to get back home and tell his mother. This was the most excited I had ever witnessed Lil Paul get in our entire relationship.

"So, your son beat you playing basketball, did he?" These were the first words I heard out of Sherry's mouth when I phoned home on this occasion, which was a week after the family visit. I conceded to defeat and expressed that I was jealous my son had better skills than I. Sherry and I both laughed, and I thanked her for allowing my son to come to see me. Sherry reminded me of this encounter that Lil Paul was still the same way he was as a little boy. I didn't quite understand what she was indicating. "What do you mean," was my reply! Sherry said in a whisper tone but with a surprising form of elation as if she didn't want anyone else to hear, "Lil Paul, he still goes off by himself and doesn't want anyone bothering him or coming in his space for a few days after he comes back from seeing you. This time it lasted longer than ever." Sherry went on to say, "it was as if he was trying to hold on to something, he didn't want to let go of," I felt honored to have had the mother of my son share this with me. I thanked her for the information and talked with Lil Paul before concluding the phone call.

Sherry allowed any of my family members or friends on my visitor's list to bring Lil Paul to visit me. From Lil Paul's ages of 3 to 13, I received an average of 4 visits a year that he attended. I would always phone Sherry a couple days following ever visit and thanked her for letting my son see me. I remembered she would share how Lil Paul liked being by himself for a couple of days after each visit with me. I played the tap back!!!! I did the best I could with the resources I had to work with. Why has this happened to me? From ages 16 to 19 I had not seen Lil Paul. I credited that to his son, Jeremiah. I pictured Lil Paul being responsible and providing for Jeremiah what I wasn't able to provide for him. He had recently graduated from High School and was making career plans. We talked on the phone once, sometimes twice a month and things were wonderful for the most part, so it seemed.

So, I stayed out of his way and never made a big deal out of his not visiting me. Was I wrong for that? This was the question I kept asking myself. Would Lil Paul's continued visits have made a difference? I decided to write him a letter that night. But, sit on it for a couple days before sending it for the sake of my agreement with Sherry. Besides, it takes two to three weeks, if not longer, for a letter to get issued in the L.A. County Jail anyway. I stayed up all night and into the early hours of the next day writing. I was housed in a single man, cell so I wasn't being inconsiderate toward a cellmate by keeping the light on. Good thing I had chosen to sit on the letter before sending it. My emotions got the best of me. I expressed some feelings and thoughts that were not wise to put on paper. I disposed of that specific letter and made a decision to write another one, which was in the form of understanding, support and concern but not pleased with his situation. There was no caution to refrain from dropping this one in the US Postal Service box because all "I's" were dotted and "t's" were crossed, "you feel me!" Even Sherry would have consented to my perceived, 'action!'

"Will the following inmate report to the control corridor for a visit, Paul Scott!" That could only be Sherry were my thoughts as I rushed inside the building from the exercise yard to get prepared. One thing I could always count on, if Lil Paul's mother said she was going to do something, it was done. However, while people may have good intentions, circumstances in life have a way of occurring that can delay, suspend and/or entirely cancel the plans made. I learned while anticipating a visit or anything else, utilize the time between so that I get the most out of the day and if things don't go as planned, I got something beneficial done from my own efforts. Therefore, my cup is half full instead of half empty.

I entered the visiting room. It was Sherry as expected. We greeted! She had a look on her face that I had never seen before. Anguish, confusion, hurt, worry and fear all combined together was the best description I could give. And, rightfully so, I could understand why. The ordeal of her baby being in the same place his father was when she was carrying him in her body 20 years ago was overwhelming. I had a long speech which I'd planned to deliver the moment we sat down. But, after seeing the pain in Sherry's eyes, my mouth was sealed and I was all ears. She poured out the hurt and fear she was feeling about Lil Paul being in the L.A. County Jail. A little guilt even came out, as well. I was not one to shoot the wounded or take advantage of a person in their vulnerabilities. Sherry knew it was her husband's responsibility to address her hurt. I assured her that Lil Paul, my son, was going to be alright. Sherry was surprised and almost displeased with me for not displaying any emotion about Lil Paul's situation. She wanted to know why I wasn't showing any concern. I had to remind her of something I wrote in a letter back in 1990. "Sherry, when I reveal my emotions, they are always taken out of context and perceived as more than what I intended. Subsequently, I get accused of posing a threat. So, I have learned how to play the game and keep my feelings concealed when I am under surveillance, around any staff and some inmates. I learned this primarily to avoid having information documented on me that the Board of Prison Terms can use to deny me parole." Paul, I don't understand?" "That's the problem! Very few do understand and those who do their hands are tied. Sherry, I am a life prisoner. Do you think this visiting room staff don't know that? They monitor my every move. In fact, the administration here probably already knows about Lil Paul being in custody and they are watching to see how I react."

"Well, would you like to know what happened?" "Yes, Sherry, please share the details." Sherry gave me play by play the complete story from the information which was given to her. In her conclusion, she advised me that because of the seriousness in the case, Lil Paul was going to have to serve some prison time. She was worried about the 10-20-life and didn't want what happened to me to happen to Lil Paul. Sherry advised me that if the court makes a plea bargain offer, which the attorney was trying to get, she was going to have Lil Paul accept it. I was not in agreement! I recommended I have a chance to communicate with Lil Paul before any plea bargain take place. Sherry insisted that the plea bargain was the best decision to make. I shared there were a number of loopholes in the narrative she just gave me. Furthermore, that accepting a prison sentence without fighting for your rights is like a person admitting to not having any rights. My first question would be to find out if any of his rights were violated. Sherry gave me an impression like she wanted to slap the taste out my mouth. What was so wrong in my requesting an investigation to be certain my son's rights weren't violated? "Nothing!" Her mind was already set on what she wanted, and I didn't realize that.

Lil Paul and I were able to exchange letters. He informed me of the charges along with the evidence. I provided him with a list of questions to ask the attorney. In addition, I flat out stated that I thought the case was very weak and would fight it. Approximately two months after Sherry visiting me, I received a letter. She wanted to notify me that my son had taken a plea bargain deal for seven years in prison. I honestly don't recall what the letter said after that. My mind went blank. I throw the letter on my bunk and left my cell. Fresh air was what I needed. Breathe, take in some deep breaths and let it go. You have no control over this. Seek Godly counsel and trust in the Lord's will and not your own." These were the words I heard in my head before the tears started rolling down my face.

At the end of work the following day, I asked Dr. Blink if I could have a word with him. "Sure, Mr. Scott, what is it?" "You might be losing me, Dr. Blink." "What do you mean Mr. Scott? You're my Kobe Bryant in recovery!" "Dr. Blink, I just found out my son took a plea bargain deal for 7 years. Wherever my son goes, I have to be there for him. I have never had a chance to be there for him in society. I'll be damned if I don't make myself available to him now." "Mr. Scott, I understand, and you are doing what any responsible father would do. For you to have been incarcerated for most of your own life, I commend you for that." "By the way, good luck!"

Chapter 3

The Inevitable

I had just returned to my cell after partaking in the last institution served meal for the day, dinner!!! Reclining on my bunk, watching the evening news on television was my usual weekday routine after work. Watching the news reminded me of something my father did on a regular basis. It was somewhat therapeutic for me because it helped me maintain an informative attachment to the community which I perceived as being educational.

The cell in which I was housed was a single man cell. The cells consisted of inside cells and outside cells; single man cells and double man cells. An inside cell faced the inside contour of the institution. Inmates who were housed in them were permitted to see their surroundings provided the cell windows were not covered by screens or paint. Those surroundings were usually the office buildings, chow hall, exercise areas and yard view overall. The outside cells gave inmates an external view of things on the outer parameters of the facility. Things like mountains, visiting areas, highways/streets and parking lots are the most common.

I had an inside cell. While lounging in what I considered my studio apartment, I heard a voice outside my window that faced the yard. "Hey Paul, brother Paul, are you up there?" My cell was on the second floor. It was this Christian brother named Joel. "Yeah, brother, what's up?" was my reply. He said, "I just saw brother Russell coming from the hospital. He asked me to tell you that your son is here." "What!!! Man, you kidding with me?" was my response. Joel shared on, "no brother, I'm not. Russell was returning from getting his diabetic treatment at the hospital and he said your son just arrived and is being processed." I thanked brother Joel and immediately commenced to get appropriately prepared. I had 5 minutes before the floor officer would be locking the cell doors and begin the 10 minutes hourly unlocks until yard recall and lock up at 9:40 pm. My mind was racing like never before. My heart started pounding as if it was going to best out of my chest. I took off the exercise clothes I had changed into after dinner. And put on my prison blues, prison uniform, and managed to exit my cell in perfect timing.

It was after the hours of regular daily activities and movement. This meant I would need a good reason for leaving the section I was housed on even though I had a runner's pass. A runner's pass was an inmate identification card, which allowed an inmate to go almost anywhere inside the prison complex on an assignment related to his work duties. If an inmate got caught misusing his runner's card, he was immediately terminated. Without hesitation, my mind said, "Paul, do this the right way!" The decision was made. I would go to the office and inform the Sergeant or Lieutenant of the situation and ask for a pass to go see my son. I went to the office, but the Sergeant and Lieutenant were both preoccupied. Apparently, there had been some kind of disturbance in the chow hall. I advised the inmate clerk that I had a family emergency and if he could arrange for me to speak with the Sgt. or Lt. His reply was, "it is going to be a while." I decided to sit outside the office complex and wait on the yard. I waited patiently as my mind began to trace the steps.

D-Quad is where I was housed, just as brother Joel. Brother Russell was housed in C-Quad. Inmates who had diabetes would go to the hospital once in the morning and once in the evening to get their treatment. Brother Russell was a diabetic and that is why he had movement. When returning back to C-Quad from the hospital an inmate could go by D-Quad if they chose. Brother Joel would walk the track on the yard most evenings after dinner. New arrivals, inmates who were transported, were always sent to the hospital for processing after getting cleared through Receiving & Release at the California Men's Colony. This meant Lil Paul was taken to the hospital after leaving R & R. While Lil Paul was at the hospital, brother Russell came through to get his usual treatment. Somehow, brother Russell found out that Lil Paul is my son. On his way back to C-Quad after getting his treatment brother Russell comes by D-Quad. Brother Russell sees brother Joel walking the track and gives him the message. Brother Joel then comes to my window and tells me. "THAT'S IT!!!! That's what happened," was my exclaim to myself. I was able to play the scenes back in my mind and follow the footsteps were my thoughts. Around 15 or 20 minutes had elapsed since the time I had initially talked with the clerk. I approached the office door again. As I glanced down the hallway, I could see that nothing had changed. My attention focused on a huge manila envelope that was sticking out of the institution mail section. My mind instantly thought, the Legal MailBox! Going to the Legal Mailbox would be a good reason for me to get out of the Quad. "Get one of those envelopes, make it look legit and tell the Quad control booth officer you are going to the Legal Mailbox." This was the conversation I had with myself and formulated the plan. I asked the clerk to give me one of the recycled envelopes. He did with no problem. I addressed the envelope up properly and proceeded to make my move. I headed toward the D-Quad turnstile exit.

The Legal MailBox was located in the control corridor. I was able to walk past the hospital corridor and look to see if any new arrivals were there. Sure enough, there was a group of individuals standing dressed in new arrivals clothing. I was tempted to go in that direction. However, I couldn't take that chance without going to the Legal MailBox first. So, I glanced and kept walking. Next to the Legal MailBox is the main control area for the entire institution. All movement is strictly monitored very carefully at this post. It is 99% of the time occupied by highly trained staff, officers, sergeants and lieutenants, who anticipate wrong before it happens. I knew my game had to be tight and I couldn't make any false moves. When I got to the Legal MailBox, I did the Houdini. As I pulled the handle on the drop box door and motioned to put the envelope inside, I simultaneously reversed the direction of the envelope and set it up the sleeve of my jacket. I closed the drop box door without any sign of anxiety. I conservatively walked away just as if I was returning from a job interview. Upon reaching the first trash can, I removed the envelope from my sleeve. I tore it into pieces and tossed it in the trash. As I resumed walking, the turnstile entrance to the hospital was about 50 yards from me. I could not resist the anxiety any longer. Thoughts commence to race in my mind like cars in the Indianapolis 500. It had been three years since I last saw Lil Paul. I didn't know what to expect. Here, my only child, who was named after me was an inmate at the same prison with his father. It was the same prison we first met; the prison where we shared our last visit, and the prison where most of our family history stemmed from, he was here!!! He was a prisoner himself, now just like his father and I was anticipating our encounter.

Up to this point, all went as if it had been planned in a movie script. I approached the hospital turnstile and entered it just as I had numerous times over the years. Upon exiting the turnstile and entering the hospital corridor, I observed a group of inmates standing outside the hospital door. They were clothed in blue denim and white t-shirts. This was an instant indication that they were new arrivals. As I proceeded with my culturally manufactured stroll, I was sure Lil Paul would recognize me. This was especially so after his observing my style of walking in and out of prison visiting rooms for his entire life. There appeared to be approximately 10 or 15 inmates in the group. Suddenly, a little short guy stepped out from the herd. He started walking toward me just as if he was taking his first baby steps. As he got closer, he extended his arms just as a child would jumping from a table into his father's arms. We both were shedding tears as we approached to embrace. The only example I can give to describe how I felt at this very moment is the story in the bible about the Prodigal Son when he returned to his father.

I have to admit that some form of spiritual intervention intervened on Lil Paul and my behalf because this was not permitted and total against the institution rules. New arrivals were forbidden to have any contact with the general population until they had been processed and sent to the Quad, A, B, C or D, in which they would be housed. However, on this miraculous occasion, the correctional officer supervising the hospital area was consumed in some other matter and had his back turned. The Step of Faith! Lil Paul saw me, his father, and stepped away from the group to greet me. I believe it was Lil Paul's courage to step away from the group that released the energy from above, which afforded us this favor.

As we continued with our embrace, grieving, and exchange of words, the correctional officer eventually realized something unusual was happening. As he motioned to investigate, the group of new arrivals cautioned him, "they are father and son officer!" Nevertheless, the correctional officer still proceeded to check things out. Once the officer saw it was me he asked, "Scott is that your son?" With eyes full of tears and a choked-up voice, my reply was, "yes sir, it is." He waved us off and said, "take your time Scott." This officer was aware of the work I did in the Psychiatric Department, as well as the ministry, and knew that I was not a problem.

So, there we were, father and son! Big Paul and Lil Paul, standing in the middle of California Men's Colony hospital corridor. We were Embracing and grieving at the same time. We hadn't seen each other for over three years. Big Paul, a model prisoner and Lil Paul, a gang member. What journey are they about to embark on? Only God knows! One thing is for certain. There is a lot of pain, hurt, anger, distrust, fear and guilt between them both.

Chapter 4

The Ultimate Challenge

The next day following Lil Paul's arrival at the institution, I served most of my sentence. I woke up early in the morning and prepared to meet him on the yard he was housed, which was B-Quad. I didn't sleep well that night. In fact, I tossed and turned all night thinking about all the times Lil Paul was brought to visit me and the different people who brought him. I did manage to get a little sleep between the tossing and turning. When I awoke from it, I was hoping it was all a dream. But it wasn't!!! This was real and I had to face it. My thoughts were becoming confusing and feelings were ambivalent. Although, there was a portion of excitement intertwined because after all, this was my son and blood in thicker than water. I said a prayer before leaving my cell and asked God for His wisdom, knowledge, power and favor in facing this situation.

Lil Paul had already let me know that he wasn't at the Reception Center Institution long enough to make a canteen draw and purchase items from the inmate commissary. I had bagged up the necessary cosmetics and some food items to hold him for a while. Plus, I had a little funny money, dollar scripts of inmate currency, to provide him in case he wanted to purchase some ice cream, sodas, chips, or candy from the mini canteen on the yard. I had informed a few of my Christian brothers and several of my comrade lifer, prisoners serving a life sentence, friends of my son's residency. However, though he meant well, brother Russell had already let more people know, then I could count.

It was a work call and the start of all inmate activity movement throughout the institution. Breakfast had been served already. I had passed on eating breakfast that day because of the overwhelming emotions I was feeling in anticipation of seeing my son. My assignment was on the yard I was housed in the Psychiatric Department. I was a Dual Diagnosis Drug/Alcohol Aide/Counselor. I had one supervisor, which was the Head Psychiatrist, Dr. Joe Blink and three inmate co-workers. I checked in at work first and informed Dr. Blink that my son had been transferred to CMC-E and was housed on B-Quad. Dr. Blink appeared amazed and stated, "so, I won't be losing my Kobe Bryant after all!" I smiled and let Dr. Blink know I needed to run over to B-Quad and take Lil Paul a care package. Dr. Blink approved and advised me to return immediately.

Dr. Blink was aware of Lil Paul's situation. Once I found out that Lil Paul had taken a plea bargain deal for seven years, I informed Dr. Blink. The following week after Lil Paul had arrived at the Reception Center, he was endorsed for the California Men's Colony-East. Now, Lil Paul was under the impression he would be at the Reception Center for a minimum of three months before being endorsed to the facility he would serve his sentence. And, he was on the bus the following day he was informed he had been endorsed. He couldn't believe it!!! "I'm going to the same prison my father is at," was what he said to his cellmate once he received the information. What had Lil Paul astonished the most was the fact that it appeared to be a dream that had come true.

"B-Quad, here I come!" It would only take me 5 minutes to get there and back to work in D-Quad. The group session normally doesn't get into deep interactions and participation until 15 minutes after it starts. I could hurry and make it back to jump right in the flow. Knowing Dr. Blink's style, I was almost certain that he would call me up and have me elaborate on my new endeavor. When I got to B-Quad turnstile to enter, I was permitted to enter with my Runner's work ID card. I could see Lil Paul standing on the yard right as I entered, waiting just as we had planned. We greeted, I gave him the care package and $10.00 in inmate currency. We chatted for a moment and made plans to meet that evening in the chapel. I departed without incident and returned back to work just as if it was business as usual. To a large extent, it was.

I made it back to work right at the 15-minute mark. The group was live and in operation when I returned. Morning check-ins to ascertain how everyone was feeling had been completed. There were approximately 20 inmates in attendance, aside from my three co-workers and self. Dr. Blink was conducting a lecture on chemical dependency. During his lectures, Dr. Blink would usually call one of the Chemical Dependency Aides, inmate workers title, up to share one of their experiences that resulted in them becoming incarcerated. I was sure he would call me up. However, he didn't! In fact, he didn't call anyone up. For some reason, he was in a zone and was not letting anyone interrupt his flow.

Group came to an end. Several inmates in attendance were housed in the same section with brother Russell. "Hey Paul, man, I heard your son was here. Is that true, bro?" This is what one inmate asked me with about five more standing right there waiting for my answer like they were in line for commissary pick-up. "Yes, my son is here," was my reply. They all had 150 questions for me following that. Dr. Blink intervened and instructed them to move on to their next program because they were delaying the setting up for ours. Two of my co-workers overheard. So, naturally, they stepped up and wanted to know the business. Before I could reply, Dr. Blink called us Chemical Dependency Aides, all together to critique his lecture and assessment of the groups mood before our next group got started. We all shared our observations. I think Dr. Blink was expecting a little more applause than what he got.

Nevertheless, we moved on and he, Dr. Blink, set the stage for me to officially inform my co-workers of Lil Paul's arrival. They were all surprised and wanted to know how I was going to handle it. The moment of anticipation!!! Dr. Blink was on the edge of his seat, fighting his curiosity for my answer. My co-workers were doing the same. It just was not as obvious as Dr. Blink. "Well, I will have to seek God's guidance like never before. For the time being, The Serenity Prayer is all I can rely on." My co-workers looked at me with complete bewilderment. On the other hand, Dr. Blink almost fell off his chair with amusement. He did apologize for his laughter and stated, "no harm intended Mr. Scott, I just wasn't expecting that answer."

Confusion lingered over me for the remainder of the day. I couldn't put my finger on what answer Dr. Blink could have expected. At this juncture, I had been employed by Dr. Blink for about 15 months. However, I did volunteer 12 step groups for his program an additional year prior to our establishing the Chemical Dependency program. The actual name was FACT, which was the acronym for Freedom from Active Chemical Treatment. Its' inception stemmed from Dr. Blink, several other inmates and myself noticing inmates with mental illnesses returning to prison just as fast as they were getting released. It was discovered that they were receiving treatment for their mental illness but nothing for their drug/alcohol problems. So, we brainstormed and designed a program that was approved and successful. In fact, it became the pilot program for the California Department of Corrections to utilize at other institutions which had mental health departments to get similar programs established. With my history being to the extent in which it was with Dr. Blink, I was just not able to comprehend his reaction. As a result, it did trouble me.

As the day grew on, Dr. Blink noticed I wasn't my typical self. At the conclusion of work that day, he had me stay back. "Hey, Mr. Scott, do you have a minute?" "Yes, Sir, Dr. Blink, what is it!" "You didn't appear your norm today and I just wanted to make sure you were alright." "To be honest with you, Dr. Blink, I couldn't understand what answer you could have expected me to give about how I'm going to handle my son being here with me." "Mr. Scott, that was not fair for me to put you on the spot like that. I do apologize and hope you accept it." "I accept your apology, Dr. Blink!" "Mr. Scott, you do know I wish the best for you. But, let's face it, there is a possibility that you won't ever get released from prison. But, right now, you have a chance to experience something that you have never had before. You never lived with your kid in society. But, he is here to live with you. I know it might be frightening. Make the best of it and don't be afraid to be vulnerable. By the way, do you know how your son got here?" "I believe God blessed me because of all the people I help." "Well, that may be true. However, I made a call to the Reception Center your son was at and

I had them clear him to be endorsed for this facility. And please, remember that we never had this conversation."

I was floored!!! Dr. Blink TKO'd me right there on the spot. Total astonishment had come over me. I couldn't wait to meet with Lil Paul later that evening. I was very excited because I knew the whole story now. Lil Paul wasn't at the Reception Center long enough to make a canteen draw because Dr. Blink made the call that got him endorsed to CMC-E. I would not be able to share this information with Lil Paul or anyone else. I had always been candid and completely authentic with Dr. Blink. Following this, I was extremely grateful and appreciative of him. Although, when it is all said and done, all the glory goes to The Lord.

Lil Paul and I meet at the chapel. It was his first time seeing the interior. Lil Paul commented, "wow, this is like a church on the streets." "Yeah, and the programs here are pretty extensive with free people coming in from society conducting them," I replied. There was a bible study taking place that evening. To avoid interrupting it, I obtained permission to utilize the outreach section from the community volunteer, John Milton, overseeing the program. I had known Minister John for many years. In fact, he was the sponsor of the Yokefellow Group I attended. I introduced Lil Paul to Minister John and shared a little history. My mother had passed away three months before Lil Paul's arrival. Minister John Milton was very supportive and influential in helping me stay strong during my mother's death. I informed Lil Paul of that right there in Minister John's presence. Lil Paul became emotional and asked Minister John did he really help me through his granny's death! Minister John confirmed and grabbed Lil Paul. While embracing him, Minister John said, "don't worry, young man, everything is going to be alright."

Seeing my son overcome with emotions like this, I began to grieve myself. Minister John instructed us to forget about the outreach section and to take the office he was assigned. Minister John walked and closed the door behind. Lil Paul fell in my arms and continued with his grieving at a much higher tone. He echoed his sorrow and pain of anguish for not being there for my mother at her dying bed. "I am sorry dad, and I'm sorry I wasn't there for my granny. I know you always told me no matter what is happening when granny comes to Pasadena to make sure I go see her. I didn't get to see her before she died. I miss my granny." I thought all my tears were gone following the mourning of losing my mother. I had even sworn that I would never cry another tear because when my mother died, so did my heart. However, God knows best, and on this occasion, the flood gates were opened once again. I could not contain myself. Tears were rolling down my face like drops of sweat. Snot had even built in my nose and I was a mess.

At this point, we had attracted a large amount of attention from the inmates who had been entering and exiting the chapel. Minister John was fully aware of everything that was transpiring throughout the chapel. Consequently, he came back to check on Lil Paul and I. It was obvious from our countenance the deep pain we had been suppressing had risen to the surface. Minister John offered to pray over us which we accepted. This was on May 17, 2001, and I still remember the prayer, for the most part, Minister John prayed over us.

The chapel program was coming to a close for the day. Lil Paul and I managed to overcome the emotions and get in some healthy father and son conversation. We thanked Minister John for his assistance and agreed to keep him updated on our journey. Lil Paul thanked me for making the arrangements for us to meet at the chapel. He expressed that it was the first time he had an opportunity to grieve his granny's death in a secure place. He shared how he thought I was going to be angry with him and was glad I wasn't. I let Lil Paul know that I had some diehard Christian brothers, as well as comrades that would be in my corner if I needed them. However, blood was thicker than water and at the end of the day we only had each other, him and I. We covenanted to make the best of a bad situation and planned to meet the weekend because I attended Alcoholics Anonymous on Friday evenings.

Chapter 5

Now's the Time to Reflect

S aturday arrived and the weather could not have been more splendid. The sun was beaming and there wasn't a cloud in the sky. I had acquired approval from my Quad Sergeant for Lil Paul to receive a pass to come to spend the afternoon on the yard I was housed. It was May 19, 2001. I never forgot this date because the majority of visits I received where

Lil Paul was present were on Saturdays. However, this was the first Saturday we visited that he was a prisoner just like me. I was prepared for us to purchase some of the snacks from the yard canteen to accommodate us while we socialized. Several of my Christian brothers and Lifer comrades would be on the yard. It would only be respectful and appropriate for me to introduce Lil Paul. Many of them will feel like they already know him because of things I have shared in groups and at church. The groups many of these inmates have attended with me over the years, 1985 to present, have been: Yokefellows, Rational Behavior Training, Reality Decision Making, Alcoholics Anonymous, Transactional Analysis, Guided Imagery, Communication Skills, Anger Management and Category X. Although, Alcoholics Anonymous and Anger Management were the only two still in existence in 2001. Very profound in-depth discussions would take place in these groups regarding issues in our lives that we were powerless over, our families/homes, and, as a result, were troubling us. Lil Paul was the main topic for many years in most of my participation. All attendees agreed upon the confidentiality code and this is what helped many inmates disclose deep personal and painful information.

Aside from me sharing my testimony in church and mentioning something about Lil Paul in it that my friends would know, I also included him in on numerous discussions when I was called up to speak during one of Dr. Blink's lectures while at work. So, Lil Paul may have been surprised by the fact that many inmates already knew him before the official introduction.

The afternoon had finally arrived! Lunch had finished being served. The yard was opened for all weekend movement and inmate activities. I was expecting Lil Paul to show up at any time now. I went to the entrance gate and waited. While waiting, I began to reflect on the last visit I had with Lil Paul. It was three years ago. He was sixteen years old then. In retrospect, I was trying to make a distinction between how Lil Paul was then in comparison to how he appears now. All I could recall was that he was distant. He wasn't his usual self. There was something that had him distracted and I never got a chance to address him about it. My mind really started wondering now and I was asking myself questions like could it have been drugs, alcohol, girls, gangs, or criminal activities. I immediately began to make a list of questions in my head of the things I was going to ask him. However, before I was able to store the second question in memory, Lil Paul was at the D-Quad turnstile making his entry.

"Hey, what's good! Did you have any trouble getting over here?" "No pop's, everything went pretty smooth." "Good! Well, let's enjoy ourselves." We embraced and went to check-in at the Quad office to make sure all necessary staff was aware of an inmate being on the yard, which was not housed there. This was a routine procedure for outer quad inmate recreational activities. Custody always needed to know if inmate(s) were on their yard from another section of the prison so that in the event a disturbance took place, they would know what measure to take. After receiving a security clearance, we purchased a couple of ice creams, sodas and headed for the bleachers.

While walking to the bleachers, we encountered several individuals who I introduced to Lil Paul. For the most part, these were convicts who had been in prison longer than Lil Paul had been living. "Wow Pop's, you know everybody!" was Lil Paul's response to the attention we received while approaching the bleachers to sit. "Well, not exactly, son. You just have to understand that this has been my life, but not my world, for the past 20 years and 14 of those years were spent here. I have seen people come and see them go. Many come back and some never get out." "What about you, are you ever going to get out?" "Yes, son, I will get released someday, provided I stay out of trouble. The slightest disciplinary infraction can cause me to receive a 5-year denial from the Board of Prison Terms, very easy. In fact, just me receiving a write up for something I got counseled on can be very harmful and result in a parole denial as well." "Sometimes son, a person can say things that will get them in trouble without them meaning to get it trouble. There are times I have to say something in my head first before I say it out of my mouth. This is to avoid things being taken out of context and it being used against you." "Lil Paul, if you don't learn anything else from me while you are here with me, son, always remember this: It is more easier for a person to perceive you as being a threat when their intentions were to keep you down in the first place. Everyone who smiles in your face don't mean you good grace." "Pop's, I don't quite understand!" "My bad son, I may have presented that too soon.

But, you are a Scott, it will come back to you when you need it. Just look at it this way, that is the Africa that's inside you and not the Africa that you've never been too."

I do have some questions for you. But, before I get started, is there anything you would like to ask me? "Yes, Pop's as a matter of fact it is! Why didn't you marry my mother?" "Son, I didn't marry your mother because of the commitment I had made to Victoria before I found out your mother was pregnant. In fact, Victoria and I had discussed making plans for a family before your mother even got pregnant." "So, did that make it alright for you to leave my mother hanging. Isn't that something you should have thought about before you got her pregnant?" "Yes, it is something that I should have thought about, but I didn't. I was just an immature youngster running around, not sure what I wanted out of life trying to enjoy every day as if it was my last. I wasn't thinking about being responsible for the decisions I made. Living what I dreamed, saw on television, or fantasized about was my driving force. I wanted what people made fun of my parents for not having and provided for me. The feelings associated with deprivation told me that I had to go get it and that is what I thought I was doing."

"When did you find out that my mother was pregnant?" "It was a little over a month after I had been in the Los Angeles County Jail." "How did you feel when she told you?" "Honestly, fear hit me like a ton of bricks when she first said it. I had called her on the phone. The moment she mentioned it, my life flashed in front of me. I had no bail charges because I was facing the death penalty if convicted on all counts. My mother and father were nervous wrecks and had to get put on medication to sleep at night. My arrest was a shock to the community because nobody thought I would ever be arrested for the charges that were placed on me. My fiancée was in her first semester of college. I had already pleaded guilty for three years on possession of drugs for sales charges, which the police found in my possession when they came with the search warrant looking for evidence in the murder. And now I'm being told that I have a child on the way. I was scared to death, just didn't die, but did hustle up, used medication to help me sleep at night because demonic warfare was coming at me from all angles."

"You know dad, that's kind of how I felt when I was in the L.A. County Jail. The difference is my son had been born and I had a chance to be part of his life before I got arrested. I have been in Jeremiah's life all the way. He will be four years old in September. He and I were really close and it's killing me not to be there for him. His mother and I got married. But, once I left the County Jail, I haven't heard from her. I don't want what happened to me to happen to my son." "Lil Paul, do you feel like what happened to me is happening to you?" "In a way, I do dad. I think if you would have been at home with me, things would have been different. My mom thought what happened to you was going to happen to me and that is why I took the plea bargain deal. But, it seems like it is happening anyway." "Wait a minute, what do you mean by that because I am serving a life sentence. You know when you're going home. I may still be in here after you get released." "You were not there for me

Pop's and now I'm not there for my son." Lil Paul started getting emotional, I was becoming susceptible myself, and I realized we needed an intermission. So, we took a refreshment break and hit the mini canteen again.

The afternoon went on, but Lil Paul and I were not able to resume our discussion. As I expected, some of my Christian brothers and long resident lifers wanted to be introduced and chitchat. So, we mingled in a civilized fashion with a twist of philosophical, spirituality and Christianity concepts sparking off in a sophisticated manner of subtle competition. This was an ideal opportunity that many inmates live for and I wouldn't dare rain on another man's parade, especially when I was in the same boat. So, I permitted some intellectual muscle to be flexed in order for me to summarize it for Lil Paul, which afforded us a chance to unite. Recreational activities came to a close. Lil Paul and I concluded our meeting and agreed to meet for the Sunday morning service in the chapel.

"Yard recall and lock up for count. Count time, count time, it is lock up for count time at the east facility," was the announcement made. I returned to my cell and could only think about acknowledging God for the experience I just had with my son. I said a prayer, thanked God and Amen. It was just closing in on the 72-hour mark that Lil Paul had been at CMC-East. I had seen him four times. We conversed about things that we never had before. We covered more ground in those three days than we had during his entire life. He obviously had been wanting to ask me that question, "why didn't I marry his mother" for a long time. I wonder how many more deep questions he wants to ask me! Only time will tell.

Count cleared and movement for dinner and the evening program begun. I chose to stay in that night. My mind went back to society. I was in the streets. Reliving my past was what I was trying to do. Only this time, I was trying to correct the mistakes I had made and clean up my side of the street. After going in circles for 20 or 30 minutes, I realized it was an impossible task. I surrendered to that fight by admitting my powerlessness to the illusion. I laughed at myself and remembered a saying, "a man left to his own devices will destroy himself." On the other hand, Dr. Blink had this saying, "many inmates' minds are like dangerous neighborhoods. They are not safe to enter at night; and not safe to enter alone." My laughter reminded me of the beautiful photographs, greeting cards and letters I had received over the years from family and friends who were dear to my heart. I kept them very neatly put away under my bunk. It was time to pay them a visit. There were some people I needed to include in on the experience I had with Lil Paul that afternoon. And, this especially meant those who were no longer with us, such as my mother, although there were others. But, my momma, was, is, and always will be in a class of her own and she gets acknowledged accordingly. Thank you, momma, for being my Angel and watching over me.

What was so apropos in my looking at photographs was that, I was reminded of a Family Visit my mother brought Lil Paul on in 1989. He was eight years old. It was at CMC-East. We were taken to the trailer, in which we stayed for two days in a prison van. Our visit was magnificent, with not a single complaint. The correctional officer picked us up in the same manner we were dropped off. When we got to the say your goodbyes area, my direction was to the right. My mother and Lil Paul needed to go left. We hugged and said our, "see you next time." As the correctional officer proceeded to escort me back into the inmate visiting process area to conduct their routine search to make sure I didn't have any contraband, Lil Paul interrupted. "Excuse me, sir, can I ask you a question?" "Why sure young man what is it," the officer replied. "Can I stay and go in there with my dad?" "I'm sorry young man, but this place is for adults only. Plus, you have to stay with your grandmother so you can take care of her for your dad." Upon the officer speaking those words, Lil Paul teared up and let out a sad, "ok." I didn't have to worry about them getting home safe because my brother June was waiting in the parking lot for them. What troubled me was hearing my son say what he did. It took ever grain of strength I had to keep me from falling apart.

Now, here I was, 12 years later preparing to become cellmates with my own child, at the same institution I first saw him at, the one he asked to stay with me and the one we last visited at. I can only imagine what my mother would be saying. In her own unique way, she had a superb sense of humor. To an extent, I could hear her voice addressing Lil Paul. But, more importantly, I could hear her addressing me.

Chapter 6

Committed to the Challenge

Monday morning arrived and work call was being announced. I expected to find out whether or not Lil Paul was going to get approved to move to the section I was housed. D-Quad was the main psychiatric section of the prison. It was designed to house some of the most severely mentally challenged, inmates in the California

Department of Corrections. The only exception for general population inmates to be housed on D-Quad was if they worked there and in order to work there you had to be housed. In most cases, the assigned work was highly confidential, and all inmates employed were considered critical workers for the simple fact we were working at the capacity of staff. I was hoping Dr. Blink could pull a string and get Lil Paul approved to move over. Otherwise, my job was going to be in jeopardy because I was adamant about being where my son was.

Business was as usual when I entered the office. Everything was set in play for us to begin the day. Regular check-ins were conducted, no concerns noted, and Dr. Blink called the first session into action. The day went great and at the completion, Dr. Blink pulled me to the side. "Well, Mr. Scott, I have some bad news for you and some good news! Which would you like to hear first?" "Give me the bad first, Doc!" "The request for your son to be moved to D-Quad has been declined because he hasn't been at the institution long enough to be assigned a job." "Ok, and what might the good news be?" was my reply. "You can move back to the general population and still retain your assignment here in the psychiatric department if you like." "Oh, wow, that will be great, Dr. Blink. When will I be able to move?" "I will inform the program administrator of your decision and it should take place within the next couple days." "By the way, Mr. Scott, let me give you a little word of advice. I would be careful who I shared any of my business with. People who, Christian brothers mainly, you thought were your friends can become your worst enemies now more than ever." "That's heavy Dr. Blink, can you give me a metaphor?" "I just did! However, just to make it more relevant and coincide with to the faith you believe. Some people don't want to see you receiving anything civilized they are not getting. If their perception is that you are receiving something that they deeply desire, themselves, they will seek to destroy you." "Ok, Dr. Blink, that language I do understand. I hear you loud and clear!" "Mr. Scott, enjoy the rest of your day and tell your son I look forward to meeting him."

There were still approximately 30 minutes remaining in the regular daily movement. I had informed Lil Paul at the end of church service yesterday that I would come to his section once I got off work. I made my move. I entered B-Quad and Lil Paul was right there sitting against the wall, which was about 50 feet away. He had a few unfamiliar guys in his company. Because I didn't have any actual official business to be in that section, I headed toward the Quad office and motioned for Lil Paul to follow. The head counselor in B-Quad was the Director of The Alcoholics Anonymous program and I could use that as my reason for being there if it became necessary. Lil Paul and I greeted and exchanged our embrace. I informed him that I would be moving to B-Quad for us to become cellmates. He was pleased to hear that and wanted to know when. I advised most likely within the next couple days. Lil Paul informed me of his talking with his mother over the institution phone. He let me know that she was overexcited and couldn't believe he was at the same facility with his father. He started the process to get her approved to visit him along with other family members and friends. He said she planned on coming up as soon as she gets approved and wanted to bring someone from my family to call me out so we all could visit together. I assured Lil Paul that wouldn't be a problem and I would give him the information to give her on who to contact to make the arrangements. Our chat ended and I returned to my living quarters.

Upon entering the building in which I was housed, I checked with the floor officer to see if I had received any mail. "No, Scott, there is no mail for you today. However, I was notified by the Quad Lieutenant that you would be moving to B-Quad after chow is completed this evening. You might want to start packing now." "Dr. Blink, put it down!" These were the words that immediately came to my mind. I was totally ecstatic and couldn't remember the last time I was filled with such joy. I didn't have enough time to get word to Lil Paul that I would be moving over that evening. My next move would be my best move! I decided to follow the officer's advice and go start packing.

One of the advantages of living in a single man cell is you're afforded the opportunity to accumulate more property than an inmate is entitled to have. I was told that six boxes of property were the maximum amount I could take, not including my television. I had ten boxes easy and still was counting. Christmas came early for some of the indigent inmates. The opportunity appeared for me to exercise a societal value. I went on a donation adventure and begun to give away things that made other prisoners think I had gotten a release date and was going home. The ironic thing about it is, to an extent, it would be home because my son and I would be living together for the first time in our lives. I did, however, leave a couple of boxes in a few of friends my cells. My plan was after I got situated in B-Quad, I would take portions of it back each day after work. Besides, a large number of stuff I had was ideal for Lil Paul to use in establishing his program. In any event, I needed to make my final round for the day because my train was waiting.

My transition to B-Quad went without incident. Although Lil Paul and I were not able to become cellmates immediately. The administration there, mainly the counselor I knew who was the Director of Alcoholics Anonymous, didn't think it would be a good idea. The reasoning was based on Lil Paul and me never living together before, me being a critical worker and Lil Paul being listed as a gang member. The administration wanted to monitor our interactions and be certain my work performance was not disrupted before Lil Paul and I would be approved to become cellmates. I could understand their point to a degree. Basically, I had worked at the capacity of a staff member in four different work assignments. At this particular time, it was my third occasion. Just to sum it up, I was getting paid per month what someone was on payroll getting paid per hour. You do the math outside the box.

The monitoring, institutionalized surveillance of Lil Paul and I took place for close to four months before we were permitted to move in a prison cell together. During those four months, we faced several challenges. We were able to bond and get to know one another better. Fear was something we had to address along with anger. Trust was a big issue that we work on with to this day. Developing the ability to differentiate a distraction from a priority appropriately encouraged us both to set goals and hold each other accountable. Lil Paul and my initial discussions were predominantly about identity, character and credibility. We only had three evenings during the week because of my involvement with Yokefellows and Alcoholics Anonymous. The weekends were more geared toward recreation, sports, activities, entertainment, social functions, etc. Although, for his first seven or eight, Lil Paul was able to do these things weekly as well because he didn't have a job assignment.

I enlightened Lil Paul of who was who and what was what throughout the entire institution. Many of the old timers, guys who had been incarcerated for 20, 30, and some even 40 years, who respected me, would pull Lil Paul to the side and share some safety preserving information with him. I always cautioned Lil Paul to be careful with who he chose to associate with. In addition, I couldn't emphasize enough the significance in his choice to pick his friends and not let them pick him. To get me off his case if I observed him slipping, Lil Paul would say, "you know everybody Pop and have friendships with them. Why is it such a big deal if I hang out with them?" "Sure enough, I know a lot of people. But I have very few friends son. There is a big difference between friendships and associates." "What is a real friend Pop?" "A real friend will not allow his enemy to become your enemy nor his problem to become your problem. However, if you are a true friend, you will find a way to assist your friend without them knowing it was you. That is a friend son because he has no reason to think ill of you." "I don't understand what you mean by that?" "Well, son, let me say it another way. There are people in life who say they are friends and know each other for many years. However, in a fraction of a second, they can become the worst of enemies. Where did the friendship go? Was it ever a friendship from the start? Son, people who smile in your face and extend their hand as a kind gesture of greetings, have motives, expectations, desires, reasons, and plans. A man who is drowning and knows he is drowning, doesn't care who he takes down with him just as long as he can get one more breath at someone else's expense. You are surrounded by men who are drowning, and they don't care who pays for their next breath. They just want to live, son, and anything that makes them feel alive or give them a bit of hope to compensate for what they missed out on in life, they try to influence and manipulate!

At that moment, Lil Paul was not able to mentally grasp many of the concepts I shared. I assured him not to worry because his memory would store it. I advised him how he would find himself in situations where it would resurface. The main thing was for me to provide him with the knowledge and wisdom he would need to survive in prison and maintain his sanity. For the most part, Lil Paul was a fast learner. It didn't take him long to start recognizing certain indications of detrimental people, inmates and staff, places and things. As time progressed with our weekly discussions, I noticed a change in his vernacular.

We, Lil Paul and I were sitting in the bleachers one evening on the B-Quad yard, sipping on some sodas just having a little small talk observing all the activities in our surroundings. We had worked out, exercised, earlier that day and was just chilling. I had no idea what was coming! I prided myself and practiced diligently in anticipating the next move of anybody I allowed in my circle. Therefore, I was never surprised when I thought someone could possibly be a friend and I discovered that they were an enemy all along. But, here I was on a prison recreation yard with my son, my guard was all the way down. In fact, I never had my guard up on him. Lil Paul hit me with the most powerful question I had ever been asked. It hit harder because I was completely vulnerable. He must have wanted to ask me this for many years. It finally came out. I guess you can say I was a cooked goose and not even the Angels from Heaven could have rescued me from this encounter.

"Hey Pop's, why did you ABANDON me?" I was in total shock and looked around to make sure we were still on planet earth. "What do you mean, I never abandoned you!" "Well, you weren't there for me." "Lil Paul, I never had a chance to be there for you son. I was arrested two days after your mother conceived you. I didn't even find out she was pregnant until over a month later. I had no bail charges on me and the District Attorney was seeking the Death Penalty." "Pops, how long had you and my mom been involved?" "I had been seeing your mother for over a year." "Ok, and during that time, she could have gotten pregnant right?" "Yes, that is correct. She could have gotten pregnant on an earlier occasion." "Well, if that was a possibility, don't you think you should have been preparing for it?" "Preparing for it! Man, I was enjoying life. I had several ladies I was seeing and in the thick of making fast money and living the life." "It could have been much better for my mom and I if you would have saved some of that money for us. It was not easy for me as a kid growing up. If you would have been there, you could have protected me from coming here." "I am sorry you feel that way, Lil Paul, and I wish things had turned out different. I can hear the anger and hurt in your voice. We need to work on that. And, I will admit there are things you have revealed to me that I need to address. Sometimes, we just have to play the hand we are dealt and make the best of it.

Yard recall surfaced. We returned to our cells to prepare for count time and evening chow once it cleared. I could not believe my son felt I had abandoned him. I thought from all the circumstances he would have understood, I never had a chance. But I was wrong, and how wrong I was. He is still a kid to an extent and very immature in certain areas of his development. A part of me wanted to defend my position and stand my ground felt like I was being accused of something I didn't do, at least to my knowledge. "Responsibility, take responsibility and become willing to be as responsible as you possibly can." These were the words that I continued to hear sound off in my head. I have to admit, during my 20 years of incarceration, I had encounters with some very ruthless convicts who wore innocent facial expressions but had cold blooded ice water flowing through their veins. I lived under a constant form of fear and safety paranoia that became normal because of the environment. At any given moment, a disturbance could have taken place. When one does, there are no guarantees who will make it out alive.

So, fear, safety, and paranoia are an adrenaline; many prisoners become accustomed to the feeling and I was one. However, when Lil Paul blindsided me with, "Pop's, why did you abandon me!", a fear came over me that I had never felt before that was in my immediate memory for recall. As a result of me being so profoundly affected, emotionally as well as psychologically, by my son asking me this question, I was compelled to do some soul searching. Consequently, a vessel was launched from my memory bank. Matthew 7:7 says it the best "Ask and it will be given to you; seek and you will find; knock and the door will be opened to you."

In 1966 my mother took me to school for the very first time. I was in Kindergarten. She had me enrolled at Madison Elementary in Pasadena, California. It was the first day of class. My mother drove me to school. As we arrived, she pulled up directly in front of Madison. My mother instructed me to exit her car and walk into the front entrance of the school and my class would be the first room on the right. Mother went on to say that the babysitter Nana would come to get me at noon and that my father or her mother would pick me up from Nana's house at 4:00 PM, depending on who got off work first. I did just as my mother had instructed me. While I was walking toward the school entrance, I glanced back at my mother as she was driving away. A deep frightening feeling came over me and these were the words that I said to myself. "Momma, I thought you loved me. If you really love me why have you brought me to this strange place and left me alone." At that moment, it felt like something had cut me in half. One side of me fell to my mother and father. The other side of me, I kept to myself.

This was how school began for me. I didn't get any introductions or tours. The only exposure I had was what I saw on television. My parents prep me the best they knew how. However, that didn't matter because when something occurred at school where I wasn't getting treated fairly, I kept it to myself and didn't inform my parents because I felt it was their fault it was happening in the first place. My thinking was if I told them they would punish me even more. The point which I would like to make here is that when Lil Paul asked me why did I abandon him, that feeling I experienced was the same exact emotion I felt when my mother dropped me off at school for the first time. Subsequently, I was able to place myself in Lil Paul's shoes, which was something I had never done before. He had a right to feel whatever he felt for me not being there because I wasn't. Although there were many issues that went unaddressed regarding my parents and my relationship, they were there. They kept a roof over my head, clothes on my back and food in my mouth. Most important, I knew they loved me the best they knew how and made sacrifices for me. I didn't get this chance with Lil Paul and he is hurt because of that. I have to find a way to help him heal first. I owe him that much. That is my responsibility. Everything else will be secondary.

The time had arrived! Lil Paul and I passed all the preliminary tests. We were permitted to become cellmates. I had been knowing the counselor since 1985, who was the Alcoholics Anonymous Director. She was in the process of preparing for her retirement. She paged for me to report to her office just hours after Lil Paul and I were finally united. She gave me an off the record knowledge to awareness talk, which immensely helped me prevail over several situations I inevitably encountered which could have destroyed me and were designed to do so. I was very shallow and naïve when I first met her. She witnessed me mature over the years and knew of Lil Paul via the times I shared about him in AA meetings she was present. She commended me for the progress I had made, encouraged me to continue living with society in focus and not to disappoint her when she checks up on me. I thanked Ms. AA Director from the lineage of my ancestry and promised I would do my best to avoid any problems.

Chapter 7

Institutionalization Reckoning

S hortly after Lil Paul and I were permitted to become cellmates, I remember a particular occasion, which was evident that being incarcerated had affected my scruples. It was in the month of October 2001. I had left the cell that morning for work as usual. Lil Paul had not been given a work assignment yet. He had only been there for five months. The average wait time to be given a work assignment after arriving at an institution was eight months to one year. So, he had the privilege of hanging out on the yard and carrying out the routine of his choice. We were developing a decent relationship, considering the circumstances. When I returned to the cell from work, I immediately noticed something out of place. My box of toothpicks was sitting there in the middle of the desk that Lil Paul and I shared. I looked the remainder of the cell over to see if anything else was out of place. The toothpicks were the only thing that raised an alarm. I placed the items I was carrying from work on my bunk and proceeded to the floor officer's desk. As I approached the correctional officer seated at the desk, I politely asked him if he searched my cell and forgot to put my toothpicks back in place. The officer advised me that he had not searched my cell and suggested I discuss the matter with my cellie if it was all that important. Talking with my cellie about this situation was exactly where my head was.

Now please take into consideration I had been incarcerated for over 20 years at this juncture. My personal property was items that I placed high value in. In fact, to some degree, they helped me feel connected to society and psychologically, I believe I was nurtured from a civilized perspective. As a matter of fact, I still had items on my prison cell shelve that my mother had sent me in the last package she was permitted to mail me from home back in 1998 before she had the massive stroke, which led to her death. Touching the items my mother sent me was like touching her hands because she took her elderly aged time to go to the stores and purchase things for me. Picturing my mother going shopping for me, picking items after items out the shelves with her hands meant the world to me. So, when I longed for my mother's companionship and wanted to commune with her, I embraced items in which she had purchased and sent me.

The toothpicks, however, were purchased at the institution canteen. I had them since 1986, which is when the facility removed them from the inmate commissary and no longer sold them. They were more like a souvenir to me and because I probably had the last box, I highly valued them. The two top shelves in the cell were Lil Paul's and the two bottom shelves were mines. I kept everything nice, neat and well in order. The toothpicks were in an area that would have been considered my imaginary vault. Seeing them on the table when I entered the cell, set off the alarm. So, I needed to find the person who invaded my space without permission.

As I exited the building and surveyed the yard, I decided to go in the direction of the exercise area. I was intensely walking past the weight pile area when a Christian brother by the name Stan Johnson hollered at me. "Hey, Big Paul, what's up, man? Where you headed, brother?" My reply was firm, "I'm looking for Lil Paul. Have you seen him?" "Yeah, bro, he over there on the basketball court. Why what's happening?" was Stan's response. I said, "Man, he went on my shelves and got in my toothpicks and didn't put them back in place." Stan immediately cautioned me and said, "Hold up bro! What you all worked up for? You mean to tell me you going to check your son over a box of chopped up wood?" Stan went on to say, "Man, that's your son. That cell is you guys' living room, dining room, kitchen, bathroom, den, and bedroom. You tripping Big Paul. Man hit the deck and give me 50 push-ups bro." Without hesitation, I complied. When I passed the halfway point doing the push-ups, I realized how foolish my behavior was. It was as if I had become more attached to the things on the prison cell shelves than I was to my own son. I was ashamed of myself and repented to my Lord for becoming blindsided by prison programming and institutionalization when I thought I had it all together. Lil Paul never witnessed any of my blurred insanity from this event. Instead, I was able to discuss it with him in a healthy manner. We both were able to laugh about it once we realized the essential elements, we had in each other. Flesh of my flesh and bone of my bone.

I did take an in-depth look at myself following this experience. Actually, it frightened me to have witnessed this behavior within myself. I knew from this ordeal that I needed to work on myself like never before. I had become complacent with the Yokefellow Group and was attending just out of convenience. Yokefellows was a spiritual counseling group headed by the Protestant Chapel. It afforded prisoners the opportunity to meet together once a week and discuss their feelings, concerns, fears and problems sponsored by a community volunteer. There was a set of rules and disciplines every member committed to fulfilling. An inmate did not have to be a Christian to attend. Off and on, I had been a member for over 15 years. At my next group meeting following this unusual behavior, I shared it with the group. There were eight guys in the group, including the community volunteer. They were all over me and could not believe something of this sort could have happened to me. However, as the weeks and months went by, other members were able to confess their own character defects. The most beneficial and amazing thing from all of this was that Lil Paul joined a Yokefellow group. The interesting thing about it, but was painful by that same token, is that I began to see him grow in many ways-- emotionally, physically, mentally, and spiritually. I saw this, but I didn't know how to fully support and encourage him. I wanted so desperately to tell him how proud of him I was, but just was not able to put it in words.

Chapter 8

The Perception

It was a beautiful Saturday morning. Lil Paul and I were anticipating visits. His mother, lady friend, and my grandson, Jeremiah, were expected to appear. Usually, on days we both were expecting visits, neither of us would go eat breakfast. We would prefer to allow our stomachs to be as empty as possible when we went on visits so that we could consume as much visiting room food as possible, thinking it was more healthy for us. When in all actuality, it was probably worst because it was purchased from vending machines only, processed foods. However, because it was something different and we could associate spending time with family in the process of gorging down as much as we could, it really didn't matter. In fact, because it was something associated with spending time with family, our thoughts were it's the best food in the world. This state of mind may have made it more nutritional for us than what was intended.

On this occasion, Lil Paul decided to get prepared first. I left the cell and hit, went to the prison yard to provide him some privacy space. The cells were not big enough for two men to get properly dressed for visits at the same time. I returned to the cell approximately 40 or 50 minutes later and commenced my preparation for the red carpet. Yes, going on a visit, and especially a nice sunny Saturday inside a California Department of Corrections Institution surely, ignited one's emotions to cause a feeling equivalent to walking on the Red Carpet at the Oscar Awards. Lil Paul was not quite finished. I just grabbed my shower gear and made my exit. While in the shower, I heard our names announce over the prison intercom. "Will the following inmates please report to control corridor for visits. Paul Scott Jr. and Paul Scott Sr." Shortly thereafter, Lil Paul walked by the shower, while I was drying off, letting me know that we had been paged and he was heading out. I immediately put a pep in my step to avoid any unnecessary delays.

Lil Paul had been in the visiting room roughly 30 minutes before I entered. Once I entered the visiting area, my grandson ran and gave me a hug. Although, it was Lil Paul's nudge that prompted him into motion. Following Jeremiah and my embrace, I greeted Sherry and Lil Paul's lady friend. They already had a table with enough space and chairs for us all to be comfortable. Sherry was familiar with the items in which Lil Paul and I liked from the vendor machines. There were already items on the table for us to consume. However, it was decided to purchase several more products before we got comfortable engaging in conversation and recreation. When we returned to our seats, a little general small talk was conducted. During our dialogue, we all agreed to play Uno. Lil Paul was seated next to his lady friend. Between Lil Paul and I, Jeremiah was seated, and Lil Paul's mother sat across from me. We played a few rounds and everything was copasetic. However, as time progressed, I began to reminisce and think about times in society when Lil Paul's mother and I were youth. Many memories of old neighborhood gatherings begin to race through my mind at the speed of light. I could not keep up with all of them and nor was I able to contain any one particular event for the sake of conversation. But all that didn't matter. Just the fact that I had an opportunity to reflect on some past experiences I had in life caused me to feel liberated, a momentary freedom!!! Consequently, my countenance started to change and Lil Paul's mother was harmony. She displayed emotions just as if we had been auditioning for a performance. The Uno game continued. But, Lil Paul's mother and I were able to maintain simultaneous chemistry.

which was evident we once knew each other. The interesting thing is that it was all innocent childhood reminiscence without any intention of crossing any lines. However, Lil Paul didn't see it that way. He requested something from the vending machines and insisted his mother go with him to purchase it. And, it was understandable that someone go with him to carry the currency because inmates were not permitted. But, his mother, in the middle of our Uno game, was a bit unusual. Besides, I was under the impression that was something his lady friend would be doing.

So, there we were, Jeremiah, Lil Paul's lady friend and I left at the table playing Uno. We played a few rounds and it was no big deal. Especially to Jeremiah because he was winning. But, when it became obvious it was over 30 minutes since Lil Paul and his mother had left the table, I needed to intervene. They were at the microwave heating up some of the items. Jokingly, I commented, "you guys haven't forgotten about us, have you?" And with a startling reply, Sherry said, "no, we were just about on our way back over there." They did have a large amount of items. Therefore, I politely gave a hand in carrying some of them back as they finished up and returned with the remaining purchase. Things resumed as normal at the table with interaction, conversations and the consumption of food. We eventually got around to taking photos, walking in other areas of the visiting room and greeting other inmates and their families who were visiting. As time closed in and visiting was coming to a conclusion, we prepared to say our goodbyes. The customary forms of departure were exchanged. The words of gratefulness were spoken and the

look of prayer for their safe return home was in our eyes, Lil Paul
and mine, as we separated and walked in different directions. Sherry,
Jeremiah and Lil Paul's Lady friend toward the Institution visitors
parking lot. Lil Paul and I back into our world of uncharted
challenges for a father and son bond.

There is a routine procedure, in most prisons, for inmates to
be strip-searched when returning from contact visits. Lil Paul and I
would always have 5 or 6 guys between us to avoid appearing in the
same group as a manner of respect and morals for a father and son.
Whoever went first, he would wait outside the building for the other
one. Lil Paul was ahead of me on this occasion. As I completed the
process and exited the building, he was nowhere in sight. I entered
the section in which we were housed and he was still nowhere in
sight. Now, mind me, the distance from the gate which I entered the
building we were housed in was approximately 150 yards. I arrived
at the cell and there he was on his bunk, laying down with his eyes
covered with a cloth to block the light out. We usually would have a
conversation after returning from a visit we attended together. But,
not this time. All the signs where there, Do Not Disturb!!!!! There is
a code amongst convicts that consist of Dos and Don'ts. In most
cases, the respect for recognizing a man's space and not causing any
disruption. This was during a quiet time of the day. Visiting was
over at 3:50 pm and lock up for count time was at 4:10 pm. Count
usually cleared around 5:00 pm. Shortly thereafter, dinner would be
served. I had a Protestant Chapel activity pass to exit the cell soon as
count cleared so that I could go early and assist with setting up for

the Saturday night service. I did not have to remain in the building and wait until the floor I was housed on got released for dinner in its' order of rotation. My plan was to skip chow once Chapel workers were released and go straight to the Chapel because I was full from the visiting room food.

Count time had begun. The evening count is standing count. This meant that all abled inmates had to be standing when the correctional officer counting came to their cell door. Lil Paul jumped off his bunk and unto the floor. We had a little small talk but nothing of substance. Something was on television which had out attention for the most part. The officer counting past our cell. Lil Paul leaped back in his bunk and resumed his meditation. It was obvious he wanted some space.

Count had cleared and the announcement was made for all inmate Chapel workers and volunteers to report to the Protestant Chapel at this time for evening services." I was a volunteer. The Chapel is opened for the general population service to begin approximately 30 minutes after the Chapel workers and volunteers are released. I was expecting Lil Paul to attend the service. However, he did not show up. The service went well, and the evening was great. All appeared blessed and inspired who attended. I returned to the cell at 9:40 pm, which was Yard Recall and Lock up. This was the conclusion for all inmate movement and activities until the next day, Lil Paul was already in his bunk sleep. I couldn't put my finger on what he was going through other than that he wanted his space. So, I didn't intrude. The next morning I went to shower the moment we were released for breakfast. When I finished and returned to the cell, he was gone. I did my normal routine. Got dressed, went and ate breakfast and went straight to the Protestant Chapel from there. Again, I was expecting Lil Paul to attend the Sunday morning church services. But, he did not show. I didn't make much of a big deal about it. In fact, I begin to reflect back when I was 20 years old and started making excuses for his behavior. The remainder of Sunday was fairly identical to Saturday.

Monday morning had arrived! I couldn't wait to get to work. I wanted to share Lil Paul and my situation with Dr. Blink and find out what his assessment would be. I went to work in the D-Quad Psychiatric Department. Once I got there, I commenced with arranging things for the Monday morning groups. Dr. Blink walked into the room and with his usual enthusiasm. I acknowledged and greeted him in return. I went on and asked if I could share something with him before the group got started. Dr. Blink's reply was, "sure, Mr. Scott, what is it?" I described Lil Paul and my distance from each other for the past couple of days along with our not interacting at all. I shared how prior, to our visit on Saturday, everything was going fine. I explained the entire visiting room experience and especially the part where Lil Paul and his mother were at the vending machines for a long time. Dr. Blink immediately broke out into a great ball of laugher, almost to the degree of uncontrollable. I took offense to that!!! Instantly, my feelings were hurt, and I took that personal. I asked him what was so funny about me sharing a hurtful situation between my son and I with him? His reply, "you don't see it! You don't see what has happened here Mr. Scott?" "See what, man what are you talking about?" was my response. Dr. Blink paraphrased the visiting room experience back to me. He specifically expounded on the part which related to Lil Paul, his mother, and I. "You see Mr. Scott, when Lil Paul noticed his mother's attention focused more on you than it was on him, at that moment his perception of you changed. You were not perceived as his father, but as a competitor who posed a threat." Dr. Blink went on to say, "your son probably has no recollection of his mother, giving you the same attention, she has given him. And, to make matters worse, if he perceived it as you are getting more attention than him, a number of concerns could have been triggered." "Well, Dr. Blink, with you saying what you have, it got me thinking. Is it possible Lil Paul could have been concerned about his step-father and mother's relationship?" was my reply. "You lost me, Mr. Scott. Can you explain?" "Sure, Dr. Blink, Lil Paul's mother, is married to a guy who my son has a great deal of respect and appreciation for. "Could this be the trigger?" is what I shared. "That could very well be true, Mr. Scott. My advice to you would be that you be very tactful in how you go about addressing this. I don't think Lil Paul had any intentions of offending you. Furthermore, has Lil Paul ever had a chance of observing you and his mother engage in any form of intimacy. And if so, how old was he?" "Dr. Blink, my son's mother, only brought him to visit me three times. The first two times he was too young to remember. The last time he was seven years old. This was the one, and only time he witnessed his mother and I engage in any form of intimacy." "Mr. Scott, for the sake of time, I will conclude with this, You have a lot of work to do on building a relationship with your son." On a more personal note, I will admit I envy you to an extent because here you are living in a prison cell with your son trying to get along. And my son and I can't get along and we live in a huge house in society. Although I wouldn't want to trade places with you! Let's get to work. Our group is waiting...

Chapter 9

The Pain of Betrayal

Things were gradually starting to come together for Lil Paul and I. We were attending Church services, exercising, going to the Library checking books out and studying. I encouraged him to devote more time to his letter writing, correspondence, and I watched how the responses he made begin to improve. He still had not been assigned a job yet. I was returning to the cell one day after having a hectic time at work, all I could think of was getting me a workout in before yard recall and lock-up for count before dinner release. Thirty minutes was all I would need. My biggest concern was to avoid getting delayed. Returning to the section in which I was housed, I had to pass the Chapels, the Library, Inmate Main Canteen, Clothing Distribution and the main corridor before entering and leaving the institution. Encountering some people, you had not seen in a long time, be it, inmate or staff. This was common to occur during this time of the day and especially in these areas. However, there was no delay whatsoever this day, and I was thankful.

I made it to the cell, all excited about getting in some exercise before yard recall. As I entered the cell, Lil Paul was sitting in the chair at the desk. He looked up at me with tears rolling down his face. He had my photo album in his lap. I asked him what was up, his reply was, "Pop's when did my mother come on these visits?" "The dates are on the back of each picture, Lil Paul," was my response. "Well, why didn't she bring me," was his response. I froze for a moment, I felt fear and it was as if I was being pushed in a corner. All I could say was, "I don't know, that is something you have to ask her." Following me saying those words, my son gave me a stare that convicted me far beyond human understanding. I can honestly say I knew how Peter in the Bible felt when he had denied that he knew Christ the three times, the rooster crowed and Peter remembered what Jesus The Christ had told him and they looked at each other in the eyes. Christ was on the cross and Peter walked away and wept bitterly after realizing what he had done. Luke 22:54-62 & John 18:13-27.

This was a golden opportunity for me to bond with my son and allow some healing to take place from some of the injuries we had both suffered. Instead, I changed into my exercise clothes and exited the cell to go get my workout in. Now don't get me wrong! I have played this back in my head hundreds of times. Knowing what I know now, I would give everything I have obtained in the fourteen years I have been in society to go back to that moment. I knew why his mother didn't bring him and not telling him added insult to injury. I could see the look of betrayal all in his eyes. But, at that point and time, I didn't know how to tell him. My son was reaching out for answers and I let him down. I wanted, so badly, to tell him how I pleaded with his mother to bring him to see me. But, for the sake of her marriage, she advised me that she could not take that chance.

So, in the letters that I sent Lil Paul's mother, the phone conversations in which we had and even the visits that I received, I tried to pour as much of myself as I could, into her, so that she could transmit it to my son and help him avoid making the mistakes with his life that I did with mine. One of the valuable lessons I learned is that a woman cannot deliver something to a child that can only come from a man. And, this is especially the case when that man is the child's father. "Bone of my bone and flesh of my flesh!"

I will admit that seeing the look of betrayal in Lil Paul's eyes not only convicted me. It also reminded me of an experience I had with my own father when I was a child. I was seven years old; this means it happened in 1968. We were at home in the living room watching television. There was a knock at the door and my father answered it. A gentleman was there trying to sell some insurance or something. My father invited him in. They talked for about 10 or 15 minutes, and somehow their conversation drifted to a television program and its' channel. My brother June and I were sitting right there, listening to everything and watching television at the same time. The gentleman mentioned the channel of the program and my father said, "my TV don't get that station." I immediately jumped up and said, "yes, it does; our television gets that station." But my father spoke over me and interjected, "I said we don't get that channel!" My brother June came to my rescue and said, oh yes, we get that channel." Our father became furious and demanded we go to our room. My brother June was 11 years old and we couldn't figure out what we did wrong. A few minutes past the salesman left, our father came into our room and said," I am going to teach you two a lesson about getting in grown folk's business." And our father gave us a good old fashion ass whooping. This was the one experience that gave me permission to lie because I didn't want to get a whooping for telling the truth. As I got older, I learned that lying was not good and promised myself that I would never mislead my children. I was reminded of this experience I had with my father because I failed to fulfill my own promise. Let's explore the dynamics and make that determination in our final conclusion. More will certainly be revealed.

I felt a strong conviction and was led into deep prayer, meditation, and reflecting on my life. I even confided in two community volunteers, Pastor Robert Bonds Sr. and Minister John Milton Sr., for biblical counsel and advice. These were two men I knew I could trust with my life and they would not lead me wrong. They instructed me just as a father would have to his own son and I was very appreciative. I, in turn, did share portions of the information I had received with my son. It opened up and an entirely new avenue for us to converse and establish an unadulterated form of trust. However, that didn't happen immediately because Lil Paul had a wall up to suppress the hurt, he was feeling.

The weekend was coming up. Lil Paul and I were expecting visits on Saturday. Our names were announced over the institution paging system for visits. My niece Sonya was supposed to have come along with Lil Paul's mother. However, something of urgency occurred at the last minute and she had to cancel. Lil Paul's mother was able to arrange for his lady friend to join her and my grandson Jeremiah. I entered the visiting room 20 minutes ahead of Lil Paul. Jeremiah was fully aware of who I was by this time.

We managed to get seats and a table in a cozy area that wasn't crowded. I had a number of questions for Jeremiah about his interest in school when he starts and the things, he liked doing the most. He liked coloring and there were plenty of coloring books in the visiting room with crayons for children use. Friends Outside made them available for children while visiting a family member incarcerated. Friends Outside is an organization that provides assistance, in a variety of ways, for family members and friends of persons incarcerated. I procured a coloring book with some crayons for Jeremiah and he went to work coloring.

It was around about this time that Lil Paul made his entrance. Jeremiah ran to greet him, accompanied by Sherry Lil Paul's mother and Lil Paul's lady friend. I remained at the table and observed as much of this rare social atmosphere as I possibly could because it was the cornerstone, aside from God, for keeping hope alive. Going on visits give an inmate the incentive to have something to look forward too. Something to value, protect and not neglect or take for granted. Lil Paul, his lady friend, and Jeremiah went to the vending machines, and Sherry returned to the table. She had numerous questions for me regarding Lil Paul and my perception of his adaption to the prison environment. I advised her that he was in the school of life and learning as he walks. That she didn't need to worry because he was going to be alright. Sherry wanted to know how Lil Paul and I were getting along. My reply was as best as could be expected under the circumstances. I informed her of his discovering the photographs of visits she attended with me and didn't bring him. She advised me that he had already brought that to her attention, and they discussed it.

Jeremiah came to the table with both arms full of food. Lil Paul and his lady friend were right behind him. Although Lil Paul and his lady friend had purchased enough items for us all, Sherry and I decided to make a vendor machine run ourselves so that we could have an opportunity to finish our conversation. I shared with Sherry some of the discussions Lil Paul and I had. In addition, I informed her of our Abandonment encounter. I disclosed how it made me feel and how I was feeling about it at this point. I mentioned that I believe things would have been a lot different if she had brought my son to see me more often. She very quickly reminded me that I was the blame for that because of the decision I made to marry Victoria and not her. I had no rebuttal for that and admitted that hindsight was 20/20. I advised Sherry that I made many decisions in which I wish I could go back and change and how it would eat me alive if I let it. But, instead, I chose to be pragmatic about life. How I, not repeating past mistakes and preparing for an authentic future was very important to me.

Sherry wanted to know where I was going with all this rhetoric. I shared how much I loved my son and how painful it was for me to be sharing a prison cell with him. I shared how much I loved my grandson and didn't want him ever to be sent to prison and that any part I had to fulfill to prevent that from happening it would be done. Sherry asked me where am I going with this; I asked her if her husband knew she called me out for visits when nobody from my family comes with her and I get to see my grandson. Her reply was no. I asked this question, does Jeremiah get to make mention of his visit with me when he returns home? The reply was I don't know because he doesn't stay at my house. I simply and politely let Sherry know on this visit that if she was not willing to let her husband know that she was calling me out to visit with my grandson when my family don't ride up with her, not call me out anymore. I felt my grandson would be conditioned to lie, keep secrets and under approved; deception harm would be done. I refused to accept such conditions and was willing to make whatever sacrifice was necessary to stand on the faith I professed. Sherry's response was that she totally understood and highly suggested I enjoy as much time remaining in the visit with Jeremiah as possible.

When Lil Paul and I returned to our cell from visiting, I informed him of the discussion his mother and I had. Prior to this occasion, but after Lil Paul had discovered the photographs of his mother visiting me in his absence, all our conversations were superficial. I apologized to him for his mother, not bringing him to visit me more when he was a child. I accepted the blame for my part and was willing to take responsibility for any damage my decisions may have caused. I let him know how much I wanted to see him and that aside from my family bringing him on visits, it was out of my control. Lil Paul wanted to know precisely what the conversation between his mother and I entailed.

Enough pain had been caused, and harm had been done. I chose to clean up my side of the story this time. I informed Lil Paul that I gave his mother an ultimatum in order to continue to call me out for visits when nobody from my family rides to visit us with her. "What was the ultimatum Pop's I stated that she informs her husband that she calls me out for visits and that Jeremiah knows who I am and spends time with me. I don't understand Pops. Why is that such a big deal? I stated "son, first of all, because it is the right thing to do. Second, it protects Jeremiah from keeping secrets and learning how to lie. I don't want that on my conscience. You see, son, I am already dealing with enough guilt, blame, and shame because of what has happened to you."

You said, yourself, that you didn't want Jeremiah to have to experience this prison life. I don't want him to ever encounter this madness either and must do what I believe is right and best to prevent it from occurring. Ok Pop's, I get it. But, don't you think getting outside of these walls as often as you can take the stress off you and helps you feel cared about. Absolutely son and that was very well said. My question to you would be, at what expense? What do you mean at what expense, there's no money coming out your pockets. Lil Paul, I was not referring to money per se. There are some expenses that money can't afford, such as your character, morals, integrity, spirit man, and soul. "Remember, I shared with you about having a strong constitution that you live by?" "Yes, I remember that." "Well, that means there are certain things that are not optional. There are lines a person set in life, and they refuse to cross those lines and insist that nobody else does either. No compromising son and not open for debate is what we have to stand on when your most valuable possessions are at stake."

"Pop's, I understand all that, but how does it relate to you just going on visits in prison to clear your head and experience a little form of freedom like you always say?" I laughed under my breath and thought for a moment of how easily one can be tested to stand their ground and represent the very principles on that in which they are trying to teach. For the most part, I had mastered this ability when dealing with convicts. But my son was a prodigious challenge. I wanted very desperately to make up for the neglect Lil Paul had endured. By doing what was pleasing in his eyes would have given that impression. However, I would have been compromising my beliefs and it would have been under the guise to please him, which would have been temporary rather than helping him acquire knowledge which would last him a lifetime.

"Son, you were very disappointed with me just a few days ago about the very thing we are discussing." "I was disappointed with you Pop because I felt betrayed." "I understand, and by all means, you had every right to feel that way. My decision now is to prevent from happening to Jeremiah what happened to you. I know it appears to be just the opposite. Jeremiah being able to see me in the presence of your mother, and you didn't, except for the three times she brought you up. By the way, do you remember any of the times your mother brought you to visit me "Yeah, I remember the last one when I was seven years old, it is funny you asked me that right now." "What do you mean it's funny I asked you that?" "Every time I see you and Jeremiah together in the visiting room, I think about that last time my mother brought me to see you."

I was not able to respond to my son, making that statement. I choked up and found myself emotionally engulfed. The institution evening count time had already cleared. Chow release was in operation. Lil Paul and I were just chilling in the cell, having our father and son discussion. But, when my son said that every time, he sees his son and me together in the visiting room, he thinks about the last time his mother brought him to see me, I had to get some fresh air. I departed the cell and went directly to the evening service at the Protestant Chapel. The interesting thing about that last visit Lil Paul's mother brought him to see me is the date my grandson was born nine years later, September 24, 1997.

Chapter 10

Adapting to the Change

S herry never gave me an answer whether or not she was going to inform her husband that she called me out on visits when members from my family didn't ride to the institution with her. At least she never gave me a direct answer. Lil Paul went on a visit the following Saturday. I wasn't aware if he was expecting it or not. He prepared for the visit in his usual fashion. Just from my own instincts, I was under the impression one of his lady friends had came up solo to visit since he had several he was corresponding with. I went to the exercise area on the yard to get a good Saturday morning workout in.

The morning went by rather quickly. It was 11:20 am, which was yard recall and lock up for Closed Custody Count Time. Closed Custody were inmates who had higher security placed on them, which entailed two additional counts each day for them. Following Closed Custody Count clearing, lunch chow release would begin, and the recreation yard would resume normal activities. After getting a good workout in during the morning, I usually went to the Protestant Chapel in the afternoon or just remained on the yard and played some chess. There was an elderly Chinese inmate named Mr. Lee, who I played in chess quite often. This was one of those perfect days for us to hang out on the yard and do some critical therapeutic thinking, which was what we considered when playing chess. Lil Paul would get a kick out of seeing Mr. Lee and I play chess because I was the only prisoner who could push Mr. Lee's bottom. I would get him so frustrated at times he would karate chop the table we would be playing chess at demanding I stop talking and hurry up and move. There were even times if I took too long to move, Mr. Lee would accuse me of touching a chess piece and be determined that I move it. He had a saying, "you touch it, you move it!" And when he pronounced it with his Chinese accent combined with frustration, anybody who heard it had to laugh.

When Mr. Lee and I played chess, we would always draw a crowd of inmates. Somehow, we had a way of creating an atmosphere of entertainment. The interesting thing, we would draw all colors, creeds, and nationalities. Though senses of humor would get displayed, an aura of peace would always be present. It was as if an invisible shrine was erected from the energy which radiated from the chess pieces and quite naturally, Mr. Lee and my personalities.

Three, four, and even five hours can go by very quickly when playing chess. The afternoon was coming to an end, and the evening was preparing to set in. Many inmates were making their last minute mini canteen runs before yard recall and lock up for count time before evening chow. As Mr. Lee and I were concluding our last chess game for the day, I heard someone yelling my name from a distance. "Hey, Big Paul, Big Paul, check this out, man!" It was a good down to earth convict I had known for many years who was serving a life sentence, just as I was. In fact, he was the cameraman in the visiting room. "Yeah, what's up, brother?" "Hey, Big Paul, I just wanted to give you the heads up, man. Lil Paul's mother was out there visiting him today with another man." I hesitated for a second and then started laughing. Mr. inmate news reporter was puzzled, trying to figure out what was wrong with me. I simply stated, "that's her husband, most likely and Lil Paul's stepfather. Thanks for the information."

The alarm sounded for yard recall. As I walked back to the cell, I thought how coincidental. I had just spent my afternoon playing chess, and I perceived Lil Paul's mother's response to the

manner in which I had addressed her that previous Saturday in the
visiting room as a chess move. What a phenomenal coincidence. I
could only look up into the sky and thank God for the signs of the
times. I will admit, my ego and pride was crushed because I had
expected a different notice to be served. This was one, out of many,
experiences where the bible became real in my life. "Be not
deceived; God is not mocked: for whatsoever a man soweth, that
shall he also reap." Galatians 6:7-9. What had went around, my
doings, it was coming back around. The good news about it, I was
able to die to self in order for God's spirit in me to live. I learned not
to take things personal. Although, they were having a personal effect
upon me, which resulted in true Godly transformation taking place.

Lil Paul had returned from his visit and was in the cell when
I entered. I inquired about his visit. He informed me that his mother,
son, and stepfather came up. I asked if he enjoyed himself and he
said yes But, it was obvious something was eating at him. I wasn't
able to pinpoint it right away. I didn't want to invade his space
because that is a total violation of the convict code, without an
invitation, when a prisoner returns from his visit. However, in this
case, it was my son. I had to bend the rule on this one and chance the
exception. I had never been faced with this kind of situation. So, I
pondered it for a moment and then took a step on trust.

"Say, Lil Paul, you seem to have a lot on your mind. Do you
need to talk about anything?" I was sitting in the desk chair, and Lil
Paul was lying down on his bunk. However, he sat upward when this
inquiry was presented. "I don't really know where to start at Pops. I

have more thoughts running through my mind than I am able to keep up with." "Well, son, that is kind of common for a prisoner when he returns from a visit. People come to visit you who love you. You get reminded of being at home with them. The visit comes to an end. They leave, and you have to come back behind the walls of madness. This environment in prison is not normal in comparison to society. You are going through an adjusting process. It takes time, and everybody has to find or develop their own strategy to survive." "How have you survived Pops? Being in prison for all the years that you have, how have you survived?" "My faith in Jesus Christ is how I have survived, son. Christ has blessed me and kept me to fulfill the calling He has placed upon my life. When I am faced with hardship, I have to remember when I address the situation, it is no longer I who addresses it, but it is Christ who lives in me that does."

"Pop, you lost me on that. I don't understand all that bible stuff you be talking." I almost took offense to that "bible stuff you be talking" term being used because I could have perceived it as a putdown of my faith, and I did notice a little aggression in his voice. But Lil Paul was hurting because he witnessed me get more excited about the bible than I did about him and he didn't understand why. That was my fault and will be addressed in chapters to follow. "One day at a time, son. I have survived by living one day at a time and getting the most out of each day that I could." "That's it right, their Pop's! I can't take my mind out the streets." I couldn't stop my outburst of laughter from erupting. But Lil Paul didn't think it was funny. He looked at me like he wanted to jump off his bunk and choke all the laughter out of me.

"Son, constantly thinking about the streets prevents one from adequately preparing for their return to them and that is why so many prisoners return to prison. Furthermore, it causes one to do hard time, which in all actuality, the time begins to do them instead of them doing time." "That's how I feel sometimes Pop's." "Well, you don't have to feel like that if you don't want too." "What do I need to do?" "Come to terms with a belief or faith in a power greater than yourself. Something that is not man made or that man can get the credit for. I choose to call mine Jesus The Christ who put together a program that helps you improve yourself in every area of your being. Take advantage of all the resources that are available to you in here use them for your good. If you do that on the day to day basis, I guarantee you won't have time to be sitting around thinking about the streets. Instead, you will be preparing for them when you get released. And remember, there is a big difference between thinking about the streets as opposed to preparing for them. Learn how to differentiate this concept and be mindful that it starts with the company that you keep.

By this juncture, Lil Paul had been at the institution with me now for over seven months. His name had been pulled to be given a work assignment. He was automatically placed in an assignment that became available in the section he was housed. He was assigned to the B-Quad office as the janitor. He worked the third watch shift, which meant his hours were from 2:30 pm to 9:30 pm. His morning program remained as it was. Only his late afternoon, evening, and night program changed. During the week, the ministries programs were the only activities available for inmates to intend in the mornings. In the afternoon, they continued along with the library being open per time divided between each Quad equally.

My work assignment hours were from 8:00 am to 3:30 pm. Monday evenings I went to Yokefellows and Friday's I went to Alcoholics Anonymous. However, once Lil Paul was given a work assignment, Dr. Blink established a Tuesday and Thursday night 12 step meeting under the FACT program, and I sponsored them. One was in C-Quad and the other in D-Quad, which were the psychiatric sections. Lil Paul was able to observe my consistency in leading by example via the productivity in my being in prison but living with a purpose.

As Lil Paul was adjusting to his new schedule, he had to discontinue attending the Yokefellow group he was in because it conflicted with his work hours. I was disappointed about this because I was witnessing his growth from being a Yokefellows member. In fact, I finally had built up enough tenacity to compliment him on the progress I saw him making and how proud of him I was. He thanked me for the compliment and advised that once he got a different work assignment that he was going to resume attending Yokefellows because he liked it. I encouraged him to make plans to achieve that.

Now that Lil Paul was assigned to work, he could apply for other institution work assignments. I talked with him about taking a

Vocational Trade Class, Computer Entry Level 1, or just something to improve academically even though he had his high school diploma. He sounded interested and stated that he would look into it. I even took him around to various departments of the institution and introduced him to staff members I knew who promised to provide him a work assignment when he was ready. Most of the Vocations, academic and work assignments which were of any significance all had waiting list which varied from six months to two years. Lil Paul did place his name on a few waiting lists while remaining in the B-Quad office janitor/runner position.

Several months elapsed and things were pretty much the constant routine. Lil Paul was receiving visits from his mother, stepdad, son, and lady friends bi-weekly. He would ask my opinion about certain things and if it were something, I could give an honest answer without letting my own prejudices dictate my reply, I would. Otherwise, I would tell him to let me think about it and I would get back to him. I continued to receive visits few and in between the visits in which Lil Paul was receiving. There were occasions when my nieces Sonya, Vicki Lynn, along with their children and my sister Ann, would come up and they would call Lil Paul out and we would visit together. There were even a couple of times. Lil Paul's mother brought Jeremiah to visit him and my family was visiting me separately, but we all mixed and took photographs together. However, when Lil Paul and I would return to the cell and have our discussions, he would always try to give me more than my share. And, he was really adamant about it when he went on visits, which I didn't attend. It was as if he conversed in a way that transmitted portions of the effect from his visit over to me. Without offending him, I had to enlighten him that his visits were for him and to be selfish with them. I shared with him that I didn't feel left out when he went on visits that I didn't go on and how happy I was for him.

It came down to me having to ask my son this question: "Lil Paul, has the thought crossed your mind that I get jealous when you go on visits?" "I know it's crazy Pop, but that has crossed my mind." "Do you know the reason why it crossed your mind?" "I'm not sure. I know that sometimes you shut down and go into your own world and you be like that for days at a time. Then you snap back like nothing had ever happened." "What do you mean I go into my own world?" "Pop, you have a way of blocking people out and avoiding them and nobody can tell what is on your mind." "Well, son, thank you for letting me know that and I will try to be aware of it. Just know that I don't ever want you to feel guilty about going on a visit or that I would be jealous. I have always wanted you to do better and be better than me."

Though things broke off in the manner which they did with Lil Paul's mother, my family, and the visiting situation all together without much being said, there have never been any hard feelings, and we all have managed to conduct ourselves like mature, responsible adults. Lil Paul did want me to attend visits more often than I did and I would have enjoyed the atmosphere. But I had to let him know how blessed I was to receive the visits in which I did. I had to let him know, "son, to have anybody come visit me after being in prison for over 20 years, is a blessing by itself that I don't take for granted. I don't look at life from what I am missing. Instead, I see life as what I can do."

Through all that had transpired from the time of my being informed of Lil Paul's arrest up until this point, I had been preparing for my parole consideration hearing. It was my seventh time going before the Board of Prison Terms. All my ducks were lined up in a completely immaculate sequence, parole plans in concrete tact, with a secure place of residence, job offers, and strong support system with numerous letters from family and friends alike. My psychiatric evaluation was favorable, indicating I would pose a low to moderate degree of threat to society if released. I had continued to upgrade socially, academically as well as spiritually and had maintained a disciplinary free program for over 15 years.

Unfortunately, I was denied parole, one more time, and found unsuitable based on the severity of the committed offense, which is what was used in all my previous hearings and was never going to change. The denial was for one year, which meant I would be appearing back before them in approximately 18 months to 2 years because of the backlog.

Lil Paul had an opportunity to witness firsthand the tightrope I had to walk and all my preparation only to encounter another disappointment. He was a bit disturbed by my frustration and subtle forms of mental isolation. Lil Paul would express his concerns and I would listen with gratitude. I assured him my mental vacations had nothing to do with him. For my own sanity, I had trained my mind to become inaccessible to people, places, and things, for whatever period of time necessary, to avoid falling off that tightrope, I had to walk.

Chapter 11

Contending with Opposition

K entucky Fried Chicken! It was Kentucky Fried Chicken Saturday and overflow for Sunday. Two to three times a year at the California Men's Colony, inmates were allowed to purchase certain items from various vendors in the community and have them delivered in bulk. KFC was one of the main sources, and the inmates looked forward to it. In fact, it was the only time of the year inmates were able to eat any fried chicken unless they worked in the main kitchen, diet kitchen, or on visits. The merchandise would be delivered to the gymnasium and arranged for distribution to individual Quads, housing section, at a time.

Lil Paul and I were housed on B-Quad, which had entrance doors directly into the gymnasium from our exercise yard. The only difficulty we were concerned about in obtaining our items was the length of the line. Usually, it was very long but worth the wait after we received our goods. It wasn't necessary for Lil Paul to order anything because I had purchased enough stuff for us both. However, he did decide to order some chicken for himself aside from my 21 piece bucket of chicken and 100 bottles of flavored water.

The process ran very smoothly and proficiently without any disturbances. However, there were a few delays for those inmates who made purchases of large orders. I had to procure a mini canteen cart to haul my bottles of water. As Lil Paul and I made our way to the building in which we were housed, other prisoners cheered us on just as if we were afloat in the Rose Parade. The 100 bottles of flavored water attracted much awareness. I wasn't the only convict who had made such a huge order. But it appeared I was the one who draws the most attention.

As we made our way to the cell, several prisoners I knew and even some of Lil Paul's homies volunteered to help. It was obvious some of these guys had ulterior motives and all help that was offered was not accepted. Lil Paul and my cell was on the third floor. The bottles of water were in 1.5L bottles, 12 in a case. This meant that a few trips would have to be made up and down the steps to complete this mission. There was no offense intended, but there were only three inmates out of the group that I trusted. One was Lil Paul's friend and the two other guys I had known for many years. One person watched the cart while the other four of us made two trips to complete the task. I gave each one of the convicts a bottle of the flavored water for their assistance which totaled three.

We managed to make room enough to store all 100 bottles of water in our cell along with our property. Lil Paul went out to the yard and had a spread, prison feast, with his homies. He took a portion of the chicken he ordered and a bottle of the flavored water. All who were able pitched in and whoever didn't was looked out for by the entirety. During food sale distribution weekends and certain Holidays, the administrations didn't make a big deal of inmates gathering on the yard with spreads and music playing. But, routinely, correctional officers would break up any group gathering based on security threat. I stayed in the cell and had my own feast. I did, however, give a couple of pieces of chicken and a bottle of water each to two prisoners I knew were indigent, had been incarcerated for many years and was not expected to get released anytime soon.

The weekend was over, and it was back to business as usual. Lil Paul adjusted to his work assignment very well. We would have most of our conversation in the cell now because of the differences in each of our work assignments and programs in general. Lil Paul was attending visits pretty regularly, three to four times a month, and that kept him motivated. I noticed him spending more time reading and his letter writing improved remarkably. I disagreed with some of the company he was keeping and voiced my concerns. We had an understanding of the access we each had at one another's property and personal items. Lil Paul knew he could help himself to anything of mine in the cell for his own use and consumption. But, if anyone asked him for something that belonged to me, they had to ask me and not him.

A couple of times a week, Lil Paul would take a bottle of the flavored water to work with him. Somewhere in the whole gamut of his associations and hanging out with the wrong people, some of them developed deep rooted jealousy. Prison politics came into play. Lil Paul was put in a situation he didn't see coming. His name came up in a discussion he felt he had to defend. Consequently, he and another guy threw blows, and Lil Paul got the short end of things.

It happened on a Monday night. I was in my Yokefellows group in the Protestant Chapel. A guy I knew from the yard had entered the Chapel and immediately after seeing me, waved for me to exit the group. I excused myself from my Yokefellow members to ascertain what was so urgent for me to get interrupted like this. The convict informed me of the situation Lil Paul was just in and advised that there were some members from the militant revolutionary organization, who didn't like what had went down and were willing to back me up if I wanted to retaliate. I thanked the comrade for the information and returned to my Yokefellow group.

This was something completely out of the ordinary and totally uncharacteristic to happen to me while seated at my Yokefellow group. The moment I walked back into the group, they wanted to know what was up. I paused for a second. Then, I hesitated before I said I don't know, I guess you can say my facial expression told it all, or at least that something wasn't right. I let the group know I had to go back to the Quad and check on something. It was only one way in and one way out of the group. One of the members put his chair directly in front of the door and blocked me from leaving. They refused to let me leave the group until I told them what was going on.

I divulged the information I had just received. Minister John Milton was the sponsor of my Yokefellow group. He pleaded the blood of Jesus Christ over me and begged me to let the spirit of God guide me through. The members of the group, seven present, unanimously agreed and simultaneously shared their concerns. It was around this time that two more convicts entered the Chapel from B-Quad and gave an indication they wanted to talk. My Yokefellows didn't want me to leave the group this time. There were about 15 minutes left before the group ended. Minister Milton liked to stay back for 30 or 40 minutes at the end of each group anyway and further fellowship because other Chapel programs would still be in operation.

I exited the group to find out what these guys wanted. Again, I received the same report as the first. Only this time, it appeared to be forceful as if my hand was being forced. I was informed that some people were waiting for me on the Quad and needed to speak with me. I thanked the guys for their information. They were under the impression I was going to walk back to the Quad with them right then and there. I stated that I would be returning to the Quad when my business at the Chapel was completed, and I excused myself. When I returned to the Yokefellow group this time, I needed to think because something was not making any sense. The first convict who came and informed me of the situation socialized with a different click than these last two characters. I realized then that it was more to this picture aside from what I had been told.

Our Yokefellow was coming to a close and they wanted to know what I was going to do. I gave my word I would seek the Lord's counsel and do what would be most appropriate for my son and I. Three of the Yokefellow members in my group were housed in B-Quad. So, we all walked back together, which had never happened before. As we reached the turnstile, I could look through the fence and see small groups of prisoners hanging out on the yard. I made my entry and was able to instantly determine who was who. One of Lil Paul's homies was waiting for me. He immediately approached and gave me his version of the story. The first convict who came to the Chapel was standing with two other convicts who I knew were members of the militant revolutionary organization. The other two characters were sitting in the bleachers with a different group of inmates who I recalled being in the gang opposite of Lil Paul.

I thanked Lil Paul's homie for the heads up and walked over to the first group of convicts. They informed me that they heard what had happened to my son and they didn't like it and would take care of it if I was willing to get in the mix. I thanked them for their offer and stated that I was putting it in God's hands. They looked at me like I was out of my mind, and I was and told me I was crazy and that they didn't offer their support to just anybody and because this was a father and son matter that they were obligated to get involved. So, they offered me their support one more time and I was told if I turn it down this time, it wouldn't be offered again. My reply was that I didn't ask for their support the first time and was going to trust in my Lord to handle the matter. A funny thing occurred here that I found to be very ironic. They became upset with me for not accepting their support. I was not able to fully understand the reason why at first. But it became all the more clear later.

I continued walking in the direction the other group of characters was positioned. Four of them were in the bleachers and two more were seated on the wall along the side of the track, which I was walking on. The track was in the middle of the bleachers and the wall. As I got closer, I realized one of the guys seated on the wall I knew. I knew he had a gang banging background. But I was under the impression he was trying to go home and let all that barbaric behavior activity stuff go. He wanted to know what was up with me once I got close to where he was sitting. I let him know I heard what had happened and was going to check on my son. He attempted to strike up a conversation with me. I let him know there was nothing else to talk about. I came to a brief halt long enough for everything that was said to be heard by all who needed to hear it and proceeded on to the building in which l was housed.

There is an instinctive intuition that a person manages to develop after being incarcerated for a length of time. It's as if you feel something in the air cautioning you to stay alert. As I entered the building, all eyes were on me. The word had already spread throughout our entire yard and was probably circulating in other sections. I was certain that custody had been informed as well. I got to my cell. Lil Paul was lying on his bunk watching television. The moment I entered the cell, he rose up and explained the situation to me. He had a couple of noticeable bruises on him. But his pride was hurt more than anything because he felt he had let me down. The things I had counseled, warned and conversed with him about the most was the exact trap he fell in. He allowed himself to get put in a spot where propaganda was used to create a situation to cause him harm and provoke my anger to become reactive instead of proactive.

By no means am I advocating this being an easy task. Make no mistake about it, l was angry when I first saw Lil Paul's bruises. But I could not afford to let anger dictate my actions. This was especially so if l wanted to prove I was ready to get released and function in society like a law abiding taxpaying citizen. My main objective was for my son and I to stay together as long as we both were in the California Department of Corrections.

I had been back in the cell for about 30 minutes talking with Lil Paul before yard recall and lock up for the night was announced. One of Lil Paul's homies came by and a few of my friends. We assured them all was well. I sat in the chair and did some deep reflection on this entire situation because things were just not adding up. It was more to the picture than what was on the surface. Lil Paul's work assignment was in the office. He was scheduled to work that day. The incident occurred during his work hours. The Quad Sergeant would have paged for him to report to work and if he didn't, the floor officer would have come to the cell and instructed him to report to work. He couldn't go to work or let any staff see him because they would have noticed his bruises and had to report it, resulting in an investigation and possible lockdown.

I had been in prison long enough, and especially at this particular institution, to know that the administration was already aware of this matter and anticipating the next move. I even asked Lil Paul how did he get out of not going back to work. He said somebody went and told the Sergeant he was sick. I asked if the floor officer came down to the cell to check on him and confirm it. His answer was no. I asked him if he thought that was a little strange. His answer was yes that that was his biggest concern and that he was glad he didn't.

I was glad he didn't come down to check also. But the point is that it was not routine, which meant there was more to the story. The other thing which continued to register in my mind was the fact that those individuals who offered me support in addressing this situation got offended and upset when I declined their assistance. I couldn't put my finger on it. But it was an obvious disappointment which appeared to be motivated by a personal profit of some kind. I slept on the entire matter and checked on my son every couple of hours just to make sure he was good.

The day was breaking through the sky. It was morning and breakfast chow release was taking place. Lil Paul chilled in the cell while I went and got some food. We had food in the cell to hold us. But I brought him a milk back and got prepared for work. I told Lil Paul to lay low and just chill in the cell. I went to work and informed Dr. Blink that I had an emergency situation and needed to talk with him immediately. Dr. Blink gave me his attention and I shared a summary of the facts. Without going into any details, Dr. Blink asked me if I would be interested in moving back to D-Quad if he could get it approved for Lil Paul to move with me. My answer was absolutely!

Following the completion of FACT first group session, the 15-minute break and the start of the second group session, Dr. Blink advised me that he was trying to get my son and I moved. I thanked him and shared my appreciation for his help. At the conclusion of the second session and while critiquing both sessions with Dr. Blink and my co-workers, Dr. Blink received a phone call. That call was from a source letting Dr. Blink know that my son and I were approved for the move to D-Quad. Dr. Blink dismissed me to return to my cell and pack up our property for the move. I left, and while in route to B-Quad, I went by the main kitchen to get some boxes to place Lil Paul and my property in. There were many boxes present. I got several of them in three different sizes, which enabled me to place them inside each other, making them easy to carry.

When I arrived back in B-Quad, I went straight to the cell. There were only three obvious reasons for a prisoner to be carrying boxes. They are as follows: getting ready to mail property home, packing to transfer to another institution, or moving to another section in the prison. Many eyes were on me again. Only this time, they were filled with more astonishment than anything else. Inquiring minds wanted to know what was I up too. I got to the cell and Lil Paul was there reading a book. I shared the plan with him, and we packed it up. We had to wait until lunch chow was over and the completion of inmates returning back to work in order for the Quad Lieutenant to sign us off and we make our departure. We were waiting patiently on the track for the office to open. We had inmates, prisoners, convicts, gang member and the works coming at us asking a thousand questions. I had already prepared Lil Paul for what we would be walking into. Our answers to every question were basically, "we don't know. They just came at us with this move out of the clear. And then we would reverse it on them and asked if they knew why it was happening? A couple of guys looked at us as if we had been reading their mail. It was evident that something was troubling their spirit. One inmate even got a little offended and wanted to know why I would ask him something like that. I simply said for the same reason he had enough nerve to come to ask me.

The Quad office opened and shortly thereafter, I was called into the Lieutenant's office. The Lieutenant asked me to have a seat, which I did. He informed me that Lil Paul and my move to D-Quad was approved and that he wanted to commend me for the way I did my time. The Lieutenant went on to say that he was aware of a disturbance that could have taken place on his yard last night and that he was pleased that it didn't. The Lieutenant asked me if I had anything I wanted to share with him. My reply was, "no sir lieutenant." As l rose up to walk out the Lieutenant's office, he made mention of one final thought. "You know Mr. Scott, there are a lot of fathers in prison for doing what they thought was protecting their families. If they were like you, they would still be at home with their families." Following these words by the Lieutenant, a cold set of chill bumps hit me like a strike of lightning from the sky. I was completely speechless but did rejoice in the spirit, and I thank the Lord for His guidance and word coming true in my life in spite of my being in prison with my son.

Chapter 12

The Chance We Never Had

D-Quad was the Psychiatric section of the California Men's Colony. On any given day, it housed approximately 800 inmates. Out of the 800 inmates, approximately 50 were considered critical workers. This meant that at some capacity, their work assignment consisted of them performing a task that made sure the program worked and was successful. In other words, we had work assignments with the duties of caring directly or indirectly for the inmates who suffered from mental illness.

Inmates who were chosen to work in these critical work assignments in the psychiatric section were screened very carefully because of the high sensitivity and possible exposure to confidential information. An inmate had to be considered a model prisoner and record clear when the background check was done. Although Lil Paul had not been in the system, prison, long enough to establish his own credibility, there was nothing in his file to discredit him. Therefore, my credibility was substantial enough for his clearance.

Aside from my work assignment in the Psychiatric Department as a Dual Diagnosis Drug/Alcohol Aide, I was a Certified HIV/Hepatitis C Counselor. I participated in workshops and speaking panels on a regular basis before new arrivals, pre-release classes, and throughout the institution. I was an Ordain Minister who was part of a hospice program that conducted monthly memorial services and counseling in the Protestant Chapel. So, there was sufficient enough information on me to approve the decision for my son to share a cell with me on D-Quad.

Lil Paul had to start out working in the Chow Hall on the food serving line. He didn't like that. But I assured him it would only be temporary. He started out working the breakfast, lunch, and dinner shifts, which were two hours each. But, after a week was promoted to a more responsible and higher functioning position, which consisted of the breakfast and lunch shifts totaling seven-hour each day. Dr. Blink was working on getting him a work assignment in the Psychiatric Department. After Lil Paul had worked in the D-Quad Chow Hall for two months, a position opened up in 'Psych Services,' and Lil Paul was placed in that slot.

Word spread very quickly that a father and son were employed by the Psychiatric Department and that they were prisoners and shared a cell together. This news bewildered many of the administration in the Psychiatric Department and D-Quad staff in general. Primarily, they were very familiar with family members on staff at the institution such as fathers, mothers, sons, daughters, husbands, wives, and on being employed there in various departments from custody, medical, education, culinary, industry, maintenance, vocational, recreation, etc. who went home at the end of their shift. But not as residence like Lil Paul and his father. The amazing thing which perplexed them the most, Lil Paul had been conceived two days before his father was arrested, and they never lived together in society.

Furthermore, this institution, The California Men's Colony, in San Luis Obispo, Ca., was where they first got introduced and became acquainted in November of 1982. Wow, despite the fact that we were inmates, our relationship and cases were good for study by the California Men's Colony Psychiatric Department, although they were discrete about it. Dr. Blink finally had a chance to meet Lil Paul in person. He was impressed by Lil Paul's manners and couldn't believe how much we resembled being brothers rather than father and son who met in prison. Dr. Blink advised Lil Paul that he had an open door pass to attend any of his groups in operation at any time, whether I was present or not. Lil Paul thanked him.

There were Physicians, Psychiatrists, Psychologists, Nurses, and even Secretaries who had never said as much as "good morning or hello" to me that were gradually coming out of their shells. They kept it strictly professional to the letter and there were no signs of ulterior motives. However, just the fact that I was getting acknowledged now by a department of staff who previously turned their noses up to me when I was in their presence was enough to inform me that something was up. I never forgot the fact that I wasn't one of them and that at any given moment, I could be on the yard pushing a broom or in a building swinging a mop, and that is what kept me in constant check and conscious of not crossing any lines.

The ultimate blessing about Lil Paul and my transition to D-Quad was it afforded us more time to talk without many interruptions, distractions, or interferences. After 6:30 pm every evening, we had the yard basically to ourselves aside from about 30 or 40 other prisoners who may have decided to hang out. Most of the inmates who were housed on D-Quad had to lock up at 6:30 every night because of their classification categories and the medications they were taking. So, Lil Paul and I would have true father and son time to discuss the past, present, and future. The interesting thing we both noticed was the differences in the conversations we had on the yard compared to those we had in the cell. On the yard, we were able to open up more and share many of our concerns, fears, hurts, pain, and even express affection. In the cell, our discussions were predominantly biblical, astrological, sociological, and political.

After the first 90 days of Lil Paul working in Psych Services, he had matured tremendously in such a short time. And it was noticeable by all who knew him and came in contact with him. This was especially so for those who visited him. However, for the battles in which I knew he would eventually encounter, we were just touching the surface of what he would most definitely need to prevail over the storms. My work was cut out for me because as I proceeded to take him to the next level, his hurt became more evident. Distrust, suspicion, abandonment, anger, hurt, and fear was written all over his face. This was my son! I had to develop a strategy to reach him without him thinking my intentions were not sincere. Trust was the biggest issue I had to address. On the superficial, he trusted me 100%. But, when it came down to breaking ground and him disclosing the Lil Paul, who was hurt because his father was not there to protect him, the wall was made of steel.

The blessing came when I prayed and decided to sleep on it. I was reminded in a dream of my father going to jail in 1966. I was five years old. The only family members who were living at home were my mother, sisters Pam and Ann and my brother June. When my mother went to work, there were things happening at our home that never would have if my father would have just been in society and not necessarily at home. My brother Vic came by when he had the time and checked on us. He even straightened a couple of dudes out real quick, on one occasion, who was flirting with my sisters even though they were welcoming it. But my father was not there, and for the six or seven months that he was in jail, I missed him deeply and didn't feel safe many days.

I remembered when my father got released and came home. He picked me up, gave me a hug, and sat me in his lap. That was the only time in my entire life that my father had ever given me that kind of attention and/or affection. I was happy my father was home and knew I was safe. I perceived my being reminded of this experience as a sign to share it with my son in the hope of it healing some wounds and help me win some trust.

Lil Paul and I were sitting in the bleachers one evening and I shared this story with him. I wasn't looking at him while I was explaining. I did glance at him off and on, however! Approximately at the halfway point in my sharing, I noticed tears begun to roll down his face. I started choking up myself and getting stuffy with emotions that were overpowering me. I managed to finish, and once I did, we just sat there totally numb, gazing in the sky as if we were waiting for a plane to come get us.

I wanted very badly to ask Lil Paul if he had ever felt that way about me. But, I didn't know how to articulate it. I had never lived with him in society. So, we didn't have a home life reference in which I could refer. He had nothing he could relate to my being there except photographs, cards, and letters. I felt sad because of that and was at his mercy to read between the lines and throw me a lifesaver by saying something. To this day, Lil Paul and I have not had any discussion whatsoever about this topic because of the pain I believe it contains. When the student is ready, the teacher will appear. Maybe this book is God's way of establishing a venue for us to embrace the pain and assist others who can relate by exploring it more in-depth ourselves.

Lil Paul had adjusted to the D-Quad atmosphere perfectly fine. The staff in the Psychiatric Department were astonished by him and had a way of making comments to pick his brain every chance they got. Dr. Blink expanded the FACT Program, where more groups were being conducted in C & D Quad, although the groups in C-Quad were for higher functioning inmates with mentally challenged conditions. More staff, mainly Physicians, either started to attend some of Dr. Blink's FACT groups, or they got ideas from the FACT Program and started conducting their own groups patterned from the FACT Program format and concept.

I assisted several Physicians with establishing their groups and was invited to speak on a regular basis. The interesting thing, I found the Physicians and other staff present asking me more questions than the inmate participants. Imagine that, I wonder why? I had no problem with complying because I viewed it as an educational opportunity for me because I was learning from them at the same time. I took all the beneficial information in and stored it in memory because I was exposed to knowledge I couldn't get anywhere else in the prison. The topics in the groups were usually centered around substance, drugs/alcohol mainly, use and abuse and how it related to developing criminal behaviors.

Lil Paul started attending some of Dr. Blink's Process Groups. These groups were designed to primarily address Antisocial Behaviors and one's failure to adapt to the structures of society. At first, he had difficulty adjusting to the group. But, after attending a few sessions, he began to see the benefit. I would always encourage him to keep an open mind and not close the door on something without first discovering the true value because it might just save his life. Patience within himself was something I saw him struggling with. I would challenge him to practice self discipline and not always give in to something just because he could or it was there. Television over reading was his biggest challenge.

There were times Lil Paul and I would walk the yard or sit in the bleachers many evenings after work and have different discussions about the things we were learning working in the prison Psychiatric Department. Many times we would get so engulfed in the conversations that for the moment, it didn't feel like we were in prison. Lil Paul would painfully admit how thankful he was for coming to prison and believed that God saved his life by allowing it to happen because of the lifestyle he was living.

Time progressed and things were developing faster than Lil Paul and I were able to keep up with. I know this may sound strange, but this is something that actually happened to me. My job became so demanding at one point where I began to neglect the bond Lil Paul and I were building. To a degree, it had its' positive points because it gave Lil Paul an opportunity to branch out and grow on his own by utilizing much of the information I had been sharing with him. I would witness his confidence increase and how he was learning to trust his own judgment without having to seek approval from others. The downside was, I was so consumed in working for the system that I failed to take the time and acknowledge his progress with a compliment more often.

There were times Lil Paul would be with me at various programs from my work assignment groups, ministering in the Protestant Chapel to conducting infectious disease workshops. The time and attention I devoted to these programs and the people I was helping displayed a more exciting attribute in my personality than what I had ever shown to him. I never had a chance to attend any of the events Lil Paul participated in as a child and got excited because he made a touchdown or scored the winning basket and I shouted from the top of my lungs with the loudest praise. I believe one of the most detrimental things a parent can do that causes harm to a child is showing more interest towards something else without first having experienced that interest with their child.

I entered the California Department of Corrections illiterate and at some point, three years later, I realized my only source of freedom was contingent on me getting an education. I took advantage of every therapy, self-help, and educational program I could to better myself. My constitution was to turn my cell into a classroom and the prison into a university. For my own maturity, production, and sanity, that is exactly what I did and accomplished. After exhausting all the programs to help me become a better person, I started helping other inmates develop hope and keep it alive by creating and facilitating new programs. This helped me feel alive, gave my life a purpose and added meaning as well as value to my name.

I wasn't able to shift from a mindset in which I had been operating with consistently for the past 18 years and just conform to a lifestyle, fatherhood and get all A's for grades. I was pushed to the limits and endured because of my faith. Second Corinthians 4:8-10 became evident in my life. Apostle Paul says in these scriptures, "We are hard pressed on every side, but not crushed; perplexed, but not in despair; persecuted, but not abandoned; struck down, but not destroyed. We always carry around in our body the death of Jesus so that the life of Jesus may also be revealed in our body."

The time was approaching for me to prepare for another appearance before the Board of Prison Terms. Hope to be found suitable for a release date was all I had to rely on. Lil Paul was growing at leaps and bounds. He was staying busy in his program and attending visits regularly. In fact, my nieces Sonya and Vicki Lynn came up to visit us with their children one Saturday. While we were visiting, Lil Paul's mother came up to visit him, along with Jeremiah and Lil Paul's sister. We had a great time together and there were no issues of restrictions. It was almost like attending a real traditional family reunion. It had been close to a year since I had seen my grandson Jeremiah. He remembered me, though, just as if it was yesterday. Everyone seemed to have enjoyed themselves in a completely affable way. I was truly refreshed and thought about God having a sense of humor to orchestrate things to happen in His timing for the good of His children.

That same evening Lil Paul and another prisoner who he worked out with challenged me and a friend of mine to a game of basketball. The best two out of three was the agreement and the losers had to buy the winners sodas. The weather was nice, what a wonderful way to conclude a day in prison after having a nice time visiting with family earlier that day. It was on! Lil Paul and homie won the first game. Pop's team won the second. It was do or die time. This was for all the marbles. Winners take all and losers go home. Though we were balling on a prison basketball court, for the moment, we had created our own world. The energy was flowing and both teams were serious about winning.

In the middle of the game, I noticed something unusual occur. The Lieutenant, Sergeant, and two yard officers were standing on the sideline, observing us. We didn't think much of it and I just thought they were out enjoying the lovely Central Coast evening weather. I mean, what else could it have been. Aside from us four convicts on the basketball court, there may have been 40 additional inmates on the yard. So, under these circumstances, there was no need for high security whatsoever. How wrong I was.

The game was over, and the Lil Paul team won. They didn't hesitate to remind us of the sodas they were expected and demanded they be ice cold. As we all were exiting the basketball court and in route to the mini canteen, the Lieutenant hurled out, "Hey Scott, big Scott, father Scott, let me have a word with you." I turned around and proceeded to walk in the direction of the Lieutenant and his staff. "Yes, sir, Lt. what is it?" "You can't do that anymore!" "I can't do what anymore, Lt.?" "You can't play basketball on my yard with your son anymore. You are here to be punished, not to have fun. I don't get to play basketball with my son at home and I'll be damned if I'm going to come to work and see an inmate playing it with his son in prison. Do you understand Mr. Scott?" "Yes, sir Lt., I understand totally."

I caught up with the guys and we went to the min canteen and got some sodas. They wanted to know what that was all about with the Lieutenant? I just said it was related to my work assignment and the group meetings I conduct. Normally we would have walked a few laps on the track and unwind from the game talking trash. But, I was a bit shaken by the Lieutenant's notice served and didn't think hanging out walking the track would be a good idea. Especially if we would have been talking trash and appearing to be having even more fun, that wouldn't have been smart. In fact, it would almost seem like I was asking for more trouble. "Not good." Besides, I needed to trace my steps and scrutinize things overall to pinpoint where this attack was coming from precisely. So, I decided to take it to the cell, shower up, and go into my think tank.

I was awoken the next morning by the bright and shining sun beaming through my cell window, welcoming me to a new day. Rather than jump to my feet and commence to prepare for a new day, I stayed in bed for a few moments. It occurred to me that I had a dream during the hours of my sleep. I didn't have the slightest inkling why this dream occurred other than that maybe God was trying to tell me something.

The dream was of an experience I had in 1971. It was when the law passed for integrating public as well as private schools came into effect. Half the children in the white communities were bused to the schools in the black communities, and half the children in the black communities were bused to schools in the white communities. I was in the group who were bused to school in the white community. The neighborhood I lived in was low income poverty stricken with a large portion of dilapidated houses and buildings. There were no gangs in my community back then. The dogs were the gangs. They ran around, terrorizing the neighborhood at night. Turning over people's trash cans and pulling clothes off clotheslines that were hanging overnight. The Street Sweeper only came in certain areas to clean the streets and that was only when some special event was scheduled to take place in the city.

When I would be riding the bus to school, I noticed the scenery would gradually change from a third world country view to the lifestyles of the rich and famous. I was only ten years old and my mind was trying to process living in a community where we made basketball hoops out of wood and bicycle rims and played drums on trash cans turned upside down. We played football in the middle of the street and didn't mind getting tackled. It meant we were tough. So, when I saw the blocks and blocks, miles, and miles of beautiful homes with the grandeur of immaculate lawns and all the plants, bushes, trees, and trimmings in complete harmonious structure, I wondered if I was in another world. Then, the basketball courts right there in the driveways and some in front yards stole the show until I started seeing swimming pools and tennis courts. I had to go to the park or boys club to see a basketball court, a swimming pool and maybe there was a tennis court depending on what park it was.

After seeing all this on the way to school, I would have to play a game of basketball just to calm my mind down and get ready for class. It was like a subtle form of mockery, humiliation or even insult for me to have been a kid living under the deprivation in which I did and be subjected to the observation of such splendor and never be officially informed of my misfortune. And the unfortunate thing about it all, I had to adjust my mind each day I returned home to what I was born in. I don't know what I felt. But, for the most part, I suppressed it whatever it was. I wanted to share this experience with Lil Paul. However, I decided to go to church and think about it.

Chapter 13

Maintaining the Faith

A fresh new week was at hand. Monday mornings were always fast. Everyone would be rushing to their assigned work destinations, inmates, and staff included, to get things in order for the week. Monday's set the tone for how the rest of the week would go. So, everyone was usually pretty adamant about staying ahead of the game. I was at work setting things up for our morning meeting with Dr. Blink and FACT's first group session when I heard my name announced over the Quad paging system to report to the D-Quad office. A page to the Quad office had priority over work. I dismissed myself and headed in that direction.

There was a distance of some 75 yards or so from the building I was leaving to the Quad office. While walking, my mind very quickly went back to that Saturday night encounter with the Lieutenant. I started wondering if this might have anything to do with it. After attending church, I decided to wait until an appropriate time to share the dream with Lil Paul that I had. The one thing that gave me a little comfort while I was walking is the fact that it was during the third watch shift on Saturday when that deal took place. This was during second watch and the different watch Lieutenants didn't get involved with the other Lieutenants business unless it was urgent. My matter seemed to be more personal than anything else with that third watch Lieutenant. So, I was able to wipe the panic from my face and look poised when I approached the office door to enter.

My counselor wanted to see me. She informed me of my upcoming parole hearing and wanted to get the process started. She proceeded by conducting her evaluation with me right then and there. She looked at what the Board of Prison Terms' reason was for denying my parole on February 13, 2002, and what they recommended I do before my next appearance. The denial was for the seriousness of the offense. They recommended I stay disciplinary free, which I had; that I continue to participate in Alcoholics Anonymous and/or other substance abuse programs and self-help groups, which I did; that I explore the committed offense in more depth via any psychiatric programs or therapy offered, none were offered. So, I complied with this recommendation by maintaining my employment with the Psychiatric Department after being employed at the capacity of a staff member for close to 3 years; and last, to have viable parole plans. Except for my current parole plans, because they can change from year to year, everything was in my Central File, which was in the counselor's possession.

She wanted to know with who and where would I be residing if released. Also, she wanted to know if I had any employment offers or possible places of interest. As was customary, she suggested I get as many support letters as possible from family and friends. Specifically, from who and where I planned to live and possible job offers. She inquired about Lil Paul and wanted to know how my relationship was with him. I advised we were getting to know each other, and I was trying to be the best father I could under the circumstances. She commended me and stated she couldn't begin to imagine what we go through on a day to day basis.

I returned to work. The second FACT's group was in session. Dr. Blink was directing the group in a lecture. I politely took a seat. The energy level was high. Much participation was taking place. I just observed and reflected on all that had transpired in my life since Lil Paul had been there with me. I was confronted by some challenges I never would have faced had Lil Paul not come there. I thought I was ready for society and all its' chaos, drama, and dilemmas. How wrong I was. I thought it was a curse for my son to have landed in prison and especially with me, when we never lived a family life together in society. However, it was all coming to me now all the more clearer. My son was sent to me as a gift from God and a blessing in disguise rather than a curse set against me.

Lil Paul was sent to help me learn the things I needed to know and develop within my character and self that the resources around me never could have before I would be ready for release to do God's work in society and stay committed.

Group came to an end and Dr. Blink wanted to meeting with all his employees afterwards which was the regular routine. However, instead of critiquing the group session like we would normally, he had some other important news to cover. An immediately to be enforced Memorandum was generated. Basically, the Memorandum implied for institutional security purposes and maintaining compliance with policies and procedures, the maximum length of time an inmate could remain in a clerk work assignment position is two years and that the policy would be effective immediately. Certain exceptions were determined by the assignment location, demand for the work, production, and how it benefited the institution as a whole.

My work assignment was in the CLERK category and benefited the inmates primarily and made the Psychiatric Department look good. Dr. Blink advised I had been employed by him for close to 3 years and would be automatically unassigned if I didn't find another work assignment immediately. I thanked him for the heads up information and went job shopping.

Surprisingly as it may have seemed, I was not the only Gold Coat inmate who was affected by this new Memorandum. Gold Coats were the work assignment smocks D-Quad inmate critical workers wore to distinguish them from other inmates and recognize them as providing a unique service for the Psychiatric Department. Approximately 15 to 20 more Gold Coat's were compelled to find new work assignments if they wanted to remain in their plush single cells. I didn't have to look very far. A position opened in the Health Education I Program for a Social Service Aide and I was hired without question. My duties were to oversee inmates categorized as DDP3, Developmental Disability Program 3 inmates. These inmates were considered to need more specialized attention and required protection from predatory type inmates due to their being more easily victimized. Therefore, my job assignment required I be very versatile in my responsiveness towards the DDP3 inmate's needs. My work hours began in the morning upon rising and usually extended into the late evening. I assisted in daily living skills and fostered independence in all areas of the DDP3's emotional, educational, physical, and mental development and sometimes even spiritual.

Lil Paul's job was secured because he had only been in it for six months. My new work assignment placed some high demands on my entire program which prevented Lil Paul and I from having our father and son talks on the yard two or three evenings during the week. Sometimes the weekends could be just as hectic, and I would have to leave the Quad all together just to get some me time. Usually, I would go to the Chapel, and even then, some of the DDP3's would come looking for me there. Lil Paul had a good way of concealing his emotions. But I knew it bothered him to see me give the DDP3's a form of my attention that I never had a chance to give him. When I would ask him about it, he would just say he understood it was part of my job description and no big deal. However, deep down, I knew it was more the circumstances just never afforded us an opportunity to address it.

June 5, 2003, crept up on me rather quickly. I was scheduled to appear in front of the Board of Prison Terms for a parole suitability hearing. This was my seventh time going before them. I had all my support letters intact. My psychiatric evaluation was favorable and stated if I was released to society that I would pose a low to moderate threat. Lil Paul and I prayed that morning and closed with God's will be done and not man's.

The hearing went as scheduled. I appeared before three BPT Panel members. One to cover the offense, one to cover my institution adjustment and the other to cover my parole plans. There was a District Attorney present to oppose my release. My attorney was seated to my right. The hearing commenced in the customary form. Each area was covered in the order mentioned above. I was permitted to speak independently following my attorney's presentation. I was asked numerous questions by the BPT members after delivering my speech. The District Attorney could not ask me anything directly. He had to refer it to the BPT Panel and one of them would ask me. The hearing reached the stage for the BPT to take a recess and for me to be brought back into the hearing once they made their decision.

My attorney and I went back into a small room, which was the same we had met in prior to the hearing starting. We wasn't there any longer than 20 minutes before we were called back on record. DECISION: The Presiding Commissioner pronounced! We're back on record and all parties have returned to the room in the hearing for Paul Scott. The Panel has reviewed all information received from the public and relied on the following circumstances in concluding that the prisoner is suitable for parole and would not pose an unreasonable risk of danger to society or a threat to public safety if released from prison. Upon hearing these words, I became very emotional and started to grieve. I don't remember understanding anything that was said from that point on. The thought of my mother crossed my mind and how desperately I wished I could have called her on the phone and shared this news. The hearing came to a conclusion. Good lucks were extended to me by the BPT Panel and I exited the room.

My attorney and I returned back to that small room. He had some papers for me to sign. But, before I did, he reached his hand out for a shake. He congratulated me and shared how impressed he was about the entire hearing and the way it went. I thanked him for his representation and departed after all business was completed.

On my way back to the Quad, I stopped at the Chapel and went inside to say a prayer and thank God for His favor. I went by Lil Paul's job after that and updated him. He was more excited about it than I was. In fact, he displayed a form of exhilaration in celebration that I never had a chance to do for him. This was another example of him helping me see what I needed to learn. And it happened on one of the best days of my life.

Following Lil Paul and my brief celebration, I returned to work. Everybody, DDP3, co-workers which were two and staff supervisors which were three, all wanted to know what happened. I gave them the good news and they all seemed pleased. There were many questions to follow and I answered them to the best of my ability. The main concern was when would I be going home. I advised there was still a process that needed to be completed. The Decision Review Unit had 120 days to approve the Board of Prison Terms decision. If they confirm, then the decision goes on to the Governor's Office for the Governor to exercise his review authority. So, I was still looking at 5 months minimum if all went well.

Word had spread that Paul Scott had been found suitable for parole. About 90% of all the inmates in Gold Coat work assignments were prisoners serving life sentences and most of them I knew. Many of us had our differences. However, there was an unspoken code that would bring us together. That code was a lifer being granted a parole date. Overnight, I became more popular than I had ever been. From the Gold Coats, to the member of The Big Four Fellowship Alcoholics Anonymous Group, Yokefellows and the overall Chapel programs, everybody wanted to know how did I do it. I stayed humble and gave all the glory to God. However, that was not appealing enough to the sophisticated intellectuals. They wanted to know what strategy of finesse did I use to persuade the BPT Panel to find me suitable for release. I topped it off with; I was honest about what I was convicted for, that I took responsibility for my actions, I showed remorse and proved that I would not pose a threat to public safety if released.

It didn't take a rocket scientist to detect that not everybody was pleased with my being found suitable for release. It became so obvious; Lil Paul was even able to pick up on it in my absence. He would make mention in the cell of certain convicts, as well as Christian brothers, attitude changes, and I would let him draw his own conclusion after establishing the facts. He was able to understand now what I meant two years ago when I shared with him that people can be friends for many years and, in a fraction of a second, become the worst of enemies. And that in most cases, it stemmed from jealousy.

Lil Paul and I were in the cell during evening count, getting prepared for chow release once count cleared. It was only two months after I had been granted parole. We were informed by the floor officer to pack up all our property, that we would be moving out the Quad. Now, for the time that we had been on D-Quad, we had several in house moves where we changed cells. Some by choice and some not by choice. But, this out of Quad move was totally in the blind.

We both looked at each other and started laughing. Although truth be told, I was pissed off initially. However, while getting my property ready to be packed, I realized something. In a few months, I was planning to do this anyway because I would be going home. So, in all actuality, they were doing me a favor.

We complied and had all our property packed and ready to go as instructed. I did have to leave some clothes, books, and other miscellaneous items in some of my friends cells to avoid being overloaded. We were moving to C-Quad, which was an extension of the D-Quad psychiatric program. The inmates there were much higher functioning. The work assignments I had required an inmate to live on D-Quad to remain assigned. Initially, no issue was made of it because I was supposed to be moved back in a week. Lil Paul's was not as demanding, so he had space to maneuver. After a couple days I was presented with the offer of moving back into a single cell. I inquired about Lil Paul and was told his work assignment was not as important as mine and he could live off the Quad and keep it. Upon hearing this, my wheels started turning and I went into deep thought. I was told if I needed to go and discuss it with my son and come back with a decision tomorrow it would be fine. I thanked this D-Quad staff member for advising me of my options and stated that that wouldn't be necessary. He wanted to know when would I be ready to move back then. My reply was, "if my son is not moving back with me, then it doesn't look like I'll be either."

I was told I had one week to find another work assignment. Otherwise, I would get unassigned and placed wherever needed. In the process of me searching for another job, I discovered that I could not just arbitrarily be unassigned without the official process taking place. I had undergone careful screening and in-depth training to secure and retain the demanding position as a Psych Service Aide. This meant that unless I was refusing to work or some incident report was generated indicating an infraction on my part, that I would have to be taken before the classification committee to get unassigned.

Nevertheless, I didn't want any trouble, and this was especially so after just being blessed with parole suitability. Therefore, I proceeded to look for a new work assignment. God always provides a ram in the bush when," we walk by faith, not by sight" II Corinthians 5:7. The interesting thing here which I perceived as another God opportunity, I got assigned to the Protestant Chapel as the Lead Clerk. Aside from the Chaplain, everything had to cross my desk and I was in charge when he was not present.

I was responsible for supervising eight inmate Chapel workers, approximately 70 inmate volunteers and the various programs they were involved, and I assisted 43 community volunteers on a weekly basis. My duties entailed a variety of responsibilities in my daily work assignment to ensure that the Protestant Chapel functioned in a safe, proficient manner. I was responsible for numerous tasks such as: checking out keys to chapel workers, the production of the weekly bulletin, Saturday evening, Sunday morning and Sunday evening services. I attended all services at the Protestant Chapel, overseeing the count of inmates attending services and documenting the total of each and how long they lasted.

I assisted with the community volunteers' programs being set up on a weekly basis to be conducted appropriately. I also was responsible for keeping track of each program a community volunteer came in to sponsor, how long they stayed and how many inmates attended on a weekly, monthly and quarterly basis. Each quarter a report would be done with all these calculations and submitted to the Community Resource Manager to show how the Protestant Chapel Program was benefiting the institution.

Shortly after I obtained the work assignment in the Protestant Chapel, Lil Paul and I were moved back to B-Quad. It took us a month to manage to become cellmates again. Many of the same individuals were still there with the same mentality. This time, Lil Paul had developed enough to recognize the cross, the double cross, and the triple cross before the deceiving perpetrators would be able to execute their plan. All the time we were able to spend in D-Quad during the evenings without any interference and/or distractions really paid off. He wasn't like a fish out of water anymore and knew how to carry himself with a persona of self-confidence rather than an appearance of naivety.

Lil Paul rejoined Yokefellows but got into a different group. I issued him an inmate volunteer pass. He got trained on the sound system and like coming to the Chapel and setting up the equipment for the services. There was an iron there also. So, he had access to ironing his own clothes and being neat for church as well as his visits. Above all, it was a nice and quiet place inmates could come and get their spiritual needs met via the School of The Bible, Yokefellow Program, Worship Services, Bible Study, counseling, prayer, watching Christian movies, listening to Christian tapes or simply sitting in a quiet place and reading their bible or spiritual commentary material approved by institution policy.

Many of the DDP3's found out I was assigned to the Chapel and it became the hang out for quite a number of them. They were upset that I left and didn't understand why Lil Paul and I got moved off the Quad. I let them know everything is not good to know and some things are best for us not to know. For some of them to just leave D-Quad on their own and come to the Chapel all by themselves was a sign of growth and showed that they were developing independence. It was evident some of the Life Coping Skill classes I had been teaching them was working. I was impressed and would complement them as often as I could.

The Psychiatric Department started making some major changes and Lil Paul was forced out of his work assignment. He was assigned to work in the B-Quad Chow Hall for starts. I helped him get changed over to the Diet Kitchen in the hospital. But, for some reason, he was unassigned from there and placed back in the B-Quad Chow Hall. It became obvious that whatever was occurring had something to do with me and it seemed personal. Lil Paul decided to get on the Vocational Electronics waiting list. In the meantime, he got assigned to the Clothing Distribution, which gave him room to breathe, leave the Quad every day, with evenings open and weekends free for visits. An inmate was not allowed to attend visits during their work assignment hours unless it was an attorney visit.

It was at the 120 day mark when I heard from the Decision Review Unit. They confirmed the Board of Prison Terms' decision. I was one step closer to freedom. There was just one more process that had to be completed. The Governor had to have an opportunity to exercise his review authority. My counselor called me into her office. This was a different counselor than the one I had in D-Quad. She informed me of how many days the Governor's Office had and at what point I would be released if there were no adverse actions taken against me.

I was within 17 days of going home from the calculation which was determined by my counselor when I received a letter from the Governor's Office of the State of California. The letter was thereby informing me that after my case had been reviewed and all the mitigating circumstances as well as aggravated circumstances were taken into consideration, the following determination was made. The decision finding Paul Scott suitable for parole was reversed and a new calendar date would be scheduled for me to appear before the Board of Prison Terms for a subsequent parole consideration hearing.

Depression hit me like never before. I went into a shell for two weeks and didn't feel like programming anymore and just wanted to shut everything down. Then, I heard a little voice saying, "Paul, it is a test! It's all a test and your son is watching you. How will he know how to overcome defeat and be victorious if his example throws in the towel. Greater is he that is in you than he that is in the world. Continue to fight the good fight of faith and know that your work is not in vain but that you will be rewarded if you don't give up and quite." I was immediately reminded of the scripture in Galatians 6:9, "And let us not be weary in well doing: for in due season, we shall reap, if we faint not." I told the devil he was a lie and to get behind me Satan because I was pressing on for the higher calling in Christ Jesus my Lord…

Chapter 14

Standing on Faith

I had been Pastor Robert Bonds Assistance Pastor over the Sunday evening services since 2000, which is the year he ordained me a Minister. Pastor Bonds was a community volunteer who came to the institution three times a week. He came on Tuesday mornings, Friday evenings and Sunday evenings. He also came on other occasions when he was led by the spirit of God. Like on February 10, 2001, the day after my mother's death. It was a Saturday. He came to the prison to check on me the moment he found out about my mother's departure. Pastor Bonds knew how much I loved my momma and what I would do to spend one day at her bedside if I could. He counseled with me that day until I didn't have any more tears to cry. Then, he prayed over me and released the power of God invested in him to continue the work that God had begun in my life until the day of completion; and that I be given the ability to endure as a faithful soldier the battle I was chosen to fight.

Sunday, February 11, 2001, for the Sunday evening service, Pastor Bonds was scheduled to bring the message. He had arrived and the announcement was made for all Chapel workers and volunteers to report to the Protestant Chapel. I was an inmate volunteer at this time. I got to the Chapel and started assisting in arranging things in order for the service when Pastor Bonds called me to the side. "Well, preacher, how are you doing this evening?" were his words to me. "I am blessed, Pastor Bonds," was my reply. "Good," he said, "and are you ready to deliver the message this evening?" was his follow through. I was taken totally by surprise. I had a great deal of love and respect for Pastor Bonds. But my initial reaction was not Godly. "What! man, you got to be kidding. I am wounded right now. My mother just died, these people are not going to let me attend her funeral and here you are talking about me bringing the message tonight. Whose side are you on because it sounds like you are picking on me just like the system has been." "I'm on the Lord's side and doing what the spirit has instructed me to do. What's impossible for man is just right for God. When you are weak, that is when Christ can be strong. Let the Lord use you son. If you have a problem with bringing the message tonight, take it up with God."

Upon Pastor Bonds sharing these words, he walked away and left me sitting at a desk with a bible open in front of me. I broke down grieving again just like the day before and for a moment, I could imagine how Jesus felt on the cross when God turned His back and all the pain from the sins in the world had fallen on Him. Then, the Holy Spirit reminded me that God had not given me the spirit of fear; but of power, and of love, and of a sound mind. II Timothy 1:7!

I was obedient and prepared the message God wanted to be delivered for His Glory and not mine. I had an out of body experience. The message was delivered by the Holy Spirit, and my situation was used by God to get people's attention and change lives for His glory. When the altar was opened for the salvation prayer to be done, there was not enough space in the chancel and altar area to contain the number of inmates who came. And yes, I was included in the count. At the conclusion of the service, Pastor Bonds kept me back and shared some important things I needed to know about the calling God had on my life and how the enemy was going to come against me to try to prevent God's work from being done.

Pastor Bonds brought this back to my attention because he was concerned about how I might react to my parole decision getting reversed by the Governor. He reminded me of how I endured my mother's loss and prevailed. Then he pointed out Lil Paul's arrival and all the trials he and I faced and was still facing. Then Pastor Bonds pleaded with me to not give up, but to hold fast to the faith for God was faithful. That God wanted to use me in a mighty way and that was why I was encountering attacks on all sides. Pastor Bonds assured me that God was going to give me favor and open the gates of freedom because there was work for me to do in society to further the Kingdom. But, that I had to pass the tests that were going to come at me.

Lil Paul was able to get a firsthand look at what had been preventing his father from coming home now. He witnessed my contribution to the institution on a daily basis. In addition, my desire to serve God and live like a normal citizen even though I was in prison. He often wondered if the powers that be will take a release date from his father while doing good, what would they do if he got in some trouble? That wasn't something we wanted to find out, though. I did notice the frustration Lil Paul was dealing with and how he would reply to things that gave me the impression he wished he could trade places with me. I would always remind him that everybody had to bear their own cross, that there were no short cuts in life. He admitted that he would never have believed the system was the way it is had he not experienced it for himself. That was the message I advised him that he needed to share in order for people to avoid making the mistakes with their lives that he did. I would let him know that God had a purpose for his life and wanted to use him to reach people through his story.

My family was worried about how the Governor's decision to revoke my parole might affect me. I assured them I would continue to be productive and do the right thing. I received a visit from my nieces Vicki Lynn and Sonya. They would always bring their children when they came to visit Uncle Paul. They called Lil Paul out as well and we had a very joyful time together. How could I not do the right thing when I had a beautiful family in the community showing me real love as often as they could. They never gave up on me or stopped believing in me. I would draw from the support they gave me when I needed some incentive to push through a day. Many times, I included them in on decisions that I made. My family gave me something to look forward to, hope for and protect. I would consider how they might feel if something happened to me or I got in some trouble that prevented them from being able to visit me. There was much more to my life than confinement to a prison rotting away. I had to see beyond the Governor's decision, beyond the adversary, beyond the circumstances and most certainly beyond the haters.

My medicine became a morning dose of a smile in the mirror, thank God for a new day, say a prayer, and read something spiritual before going to work. I stopped thinking about freedom and commenced to living as if I was free. Lil Paul's program was going great. He had two years left to serve on his sentence before the gates would open and there would be light. Our first two years went by very quickly. We used to sit in the cell and have discussions reminiscing on the past and thanking God for keeping us together throughout all the trials we faced. I would remind him that our journey was not over, and we still had some mountains to climb. He would laugh as if he knew something that he didn't. "The hard part is done Pops. It's behind us now, and we have a future to look forward too. Doesn't Isaiah 40:31 say, but those who hope in the Lord will renew their strength. They will soar on wings like eagles; they will run and not grow weary; they will walk and not be faint?" "Yes, son, that's what it says! I see you've been studying." "Well, like you say Pops, stay ready, so you don't have to get ready."

I had no idea where Lil Paul had gotten this insight from. I definitely couldn't take the credit for it. I knew he was attending Yokefellows regular, worship service and School of the Bible. That was it, School of The Bible or some of those counseling sessions with Minister John Milton or Pastor Bonds. Either way, I was impressed as well as inspired. He was coming into his own and learning how to use the word of God in conversations appropriately. He was on track to start testifying about God's goodness, mercy, and grace.

The Protestant Chapel Programs were growing unbelievably. Every day during the week, except for Friday's, there was a program available to the inmate population in the mornings, afternoons and evenings, to meet their spiritual needs. Once a month Memorial Services were conducted. The Memorial Services were initially set up for inmates who passed away at the California Men's Colony. However, because there were a number of inmates who had relatives in society that were departing, many unexpectedly, and they were not able to attend their family members Home Going in the community, such cases were permitted to honor their loved ones in the monthly Memorial Services as well.

The Chaplain, who preferred to be called Reverend, had a heart for doing the will of God. Many times, he would go above and beyond to make sure as many programs stayed in operation as possible because he knew the Protestant Chapel was as close to freedom many of the inmates housed at CMC-East were ever going to get. The Reverend had a great sense of humor and would periodically make comments that he was serving a life sentence along with us. The Reverend would read a book a week and one extra every time he was scheduled to bring the message. I remember a saying the Reverend would hit me with on seldom occasions: He would say, "Paul, would you rather fail at something you eventually succeeded at; or would you rather succeed at something you eventually failed at?" In the early '90s, when the Rev. first asked me that, I had to scratch my head and tell the Rev. I would get back to him on that. In the late '90s, when the Rev. asked me that, my answer was the first. I would rather fail at something I eventually succeeded at! In 2004 when the Rev. asked me this same question, my answer was as follows: "Rev. I count it all joy for the sake of Christ if I can just finish this race He has called me to run." The Rev. didn't say a word. Instead, he embraced me and opened his office door for me to walk out and another prisoner to walk in.

Not long after the Reverend and I had what I termed, 'The encounter with Jesus the Messiah' Matthew 16:13-20, he was faced with a challenging assignment, and the Protestant Chapel Program was in jeopardy. Avenal State Prison in Kings County California was in need of a Chaplain fill in until they got a permanent Chaplain on staff. The Protestant Chaplain from the California Men's Colony was selected. The Community Resource Manager was contemplating suspending portions if not all of the Protestant Chapel Programs until the Chaplain returned from the assignment at Avenal State Prison. Without hesitation, Chaplain asked the Community Resource Manager to let inmate Paul Scott run the Protestant Chapel Program in his absence. The Community Resource Manager asked the Chaplain if he knew what he was asking of to be done. That nothing of such had ever taken place at the California Men's Colony and that if anything went wrong, it could possibly cost him his job. The Chaplain said I think he will do a good job.

The Chaplain's request was granted, and I was in the driver's seat of the Protestant Chapel Program for 79 days, which is when the Chaplain returned. Not one single incident occurred during the Chaplain's absence and everything ran just as if he had never left. The Community Resource Manager couldn't believe it and the Chaplain was pleased. I thanked the Chaplain for trusting me to represent him at such a level and for the opportunity to honor my Lord. The Chaplain was discerning enough to differentiate between who was reading the bible as opposed to who was living it. My biggest blessings from the Rev., who was the Chaplain, is that he taught me the true meaning in being a Chaplain and how to keep Chaplaincy separated from denominations, doctrine, dogmas and deception. How can I say I love a God who I don't see if I can't show compassion toward another human being suffering who I do see.

Chapter 15

Restoration

The afternoon was full with radiance of beauty twinkling in from the sky that reflected a facet of creation that man could only enjoy but never get the credit for existing. It was a Saturday to be precise. Lil Paul was on a visit, and I was seated on a stool at the Protestant Chapel door. I was waiting for the Seventh-day Adventist community volunteers to come in and start their service. While sitting there waiting I had a revelation.

The spirit of God fell on me like a raindrop from the clouds. I saw myself going back before the Board of Prison Terms. They found me suitable for parole again and all processes were favorable, and I got released. Shortly before I discharged, parole Pastor Robert Bonds obtained full time employment as a Chaplain in the California Department of Corrections, which he had been trying for over 16 years before finally getting in. Once my parole was discharged, Pastor Bonds, now Chaplain Bonds, got me approved to enter his facility and share my testimony and preach the word.

The Seventh-day Adventist arrived, I set things up for their program and didn't think much more about the revelation. I didn't share it with anyone either. Everything was business as usual. Preparation for the Christmas Family Service was getting close. Many inmates were signing up. But, only the first 50 who got randomly chosen by the Chaplain were selected. The Christmas Family Service for the Protestant Chapel was an event held on a Saturday. A prisoner was permitted to invite one, maybe two and sometimes three immediate family members, adults only, inside the institution to the Protestant Chapel. They would attend a church service and partake in a banquet kind of celebration thereafter. The Christmas Family Service was very instrumental in supporting many families and keeping them together. The Seventh-day Adventist community volunteers were interested in attending and wanted to know what the process entailed.

My being at the Chapel had not only become my work assignment. It became my world. I was there seven days a week on an average of eight hours daily. I usually got my workout in early in the morning before going to work. A support group for inmates who were infected with HIV/AIDS and/or Hepatitis was established because of the request for individual counseling increasing. The Rev. didn't believe in any inmates being turned away from the Protestant Chapel, who came there with a legitimate need. The program was constantly expanding to fulfill the Mission Statement, Address the spiritual needs of the inmate population.

Pastor Bonds wanted me to schedule a Baptism Service for him. In his making mention of it to me, he emphasized that it was going to be a very special one. All the arrangements were made, and everything was placed in order. There was a one session class that all interested parties had to attend. Lil Paul was in the lineup. He was maturing by the days and it truly was a blessing to see my son growing right before my eyes even if we were in prison.

The Baptism day arrived. I always assisted Pastor Bonds during the Baptism and nothing had changed this time except one thing. When the time came for Paul Darryl Scott Jr. to be submerged into the pool of water as the old, and rising up washed anew as a symbolic public witness that the old man died with Christ and the new arose to life, Pastor Bonds gave me, Paul Darryl Scott Sr. the honors of carrying out the mission. "Please pronounce your name?" "Paul Darryl Scott Jr." "Paul Darryl Scott Jr., have you accepted Jesus Christ as your Lord and Savior?" "Yes, I have!" "Do you believe that Jesus Christ lived here on earth, was persecuted for your sins, died, resurrected and sits at the right hand of His Father in Heaven?" "I do!" By the confession of your faith and the power invested in me, I now baptize you in the name of the Father, the Son, and the Holy Spirit. Good thing we were last because the whole Chapel lit up light Times Square acknowledging what the King of all Kings and Lord of all Lords commanded the believers to do in His name.

In the process of everything going well, I had a Glaucoma flare up in my right eye. I was diagnosed with Open Angle Glaucoma in October of 1988. The pressure in my right eye was at an unusual high level in April of 1991, and laser surgery had to be performed to get the pressure under control. I had no problems with controlling the pressures from that time until there in late November 2004. I was taken to the office of a private ophthalmologist to have the Laser surgery done for the second time in my right eye. I was told by the physician that one of the side effects of having Laser surgery done a second time in the same eye is the pressure can leap very high and other procedures have to be taken immediately.

Unfortunately, that is what happened in my case. I was taken to the French Medical Center in San Luis Obispo, California, and had a more delicate surgical procedure done. When examined the next day, it was determined that another surgery needed to be done immediately to prevent my right eye from going totally blind. This procedure still did not correct the problem. I encountered another set of adverse effects that I had to endure. After the fourth surgery, the pressure on my right optic nerve was back under control. I had been taken to medical facilities in society for five days in a roll. The view of society was nice and especially when I was able to see the ocean coastline. But, after five days in a roll and all the doctoring that was being done on me, I was beat, and fatigue had resided in me. I needed some rest and my body forced me to take a weekend off and stay in the cell the entire time. The only time I had ever done this during the current 24 years I had served, was in 1982 when I was in the hole, and the few times the institution was on lockdowns, which was few and in between. So, it wasn't something I was used to. Nevertheless, my body didn't complain one bit; although, my mind was all over the place.

The time had arrived for me to prepare for the Board of Prison Terms one more time. I informed my family and friends. Not long thereafter, my support letters started rolling in. My first cousin, Keith Bowen Sr., who was a Los Angeles County Sheriff Deputy had provided me with a letter of support just as he did for my previous hearing. Only this time, he included some extra help. His mother-in-law, at that time, Councilwoman Marcine Shaw, had offered a letter of support for parole on my behalf as well. Marcine Shaw had served eight years in the City of Compton as a councilperson, over 20 years working for the Los Angeles County Board of Supervisors, continued to serve as a Los Angeles County Commission for the Department of Social Services and played a very vital part in the Special Olympics being established and supported.

The closer Lil Paul got to his release date, the more I noticed he was careful about having conversations with me about the free world. By this time, he had 18 months left on his sentence. The letters started coming in more frequent, quite frequent, as a matter of fact. He was going on visits more often. He had a couple of his lady friends re-establish communication with him and wanted to come to visit him. He was reluctant because he already had a lady visiting him and he didn't want to take a chance of them clashing in the visiting room. He finally got around to sharing it with me and asking my opinion once he realized it wouldn't hurt my feelings to partake in such a discussion because he knew when he was going home and I didn't.

Lil Paul wanted to know what would I do if I were in his shoes. I let him know I didn't have enough information to put myself in his shoes. He wanted to know what I meant by that. "Well, the first lady who has already been coming to see you, is she your friend, your lady, or has any plans or promises been discussed that you don't plan on sticking to your end of the agreement?" "No, Pops, we just friends. She helps me out with a little money here and there, but we are just friends." "Ok, do you think it would offend her if you had another friend who begun to do the things for you that she does?" "I don't know, I never thought about it." "That's the problem, son! We say we don't know and that we never thought about it. But, you already know what the answer is." "What you mean by that?" "Come on, Lil Paul, whether you have talked with her about it or not, that woman coming to see you and putting money on your books is in expectation and anticipation of something, don't you think?" "Since you put it that way, I guess so." "Ok, so quite naturally, a person will be alarmed by something they perceive is going to interfere or block what they are expecting and anticipating." "Ok Pops, so what would you do if you were in my shoes?"

"Lil Paul, you, my son, and I love you. But, I can't put myself in your shoes on this one. I can only speak of what I would do if I was in the situation myself." "No problem Pops, what would you do?" "On my next visit I would let her know a few old friends of mine contacted me and I sent them the information to get approved to come visit me. A real friend with no ulterior motives wouldn't have a problem with that. I would observe her response to this and proceed from there. Bottom line is I haven't made a commitment to anyone which leaves my options open. Until something serious gets discussed, I will have some friends coming to visit me while I am locked up in prison. Now, if one of them has some kind of personal agenda for whatever reason(s) that they haven't discussed with me, it will reveal itself and that will be to my best interest because it will expose their hand and plan. Better to find out before you get out whether you can trust a person or not"

Lil Paul, my best advice to you is never deny yourself the opportunity to experience what will help you grow and become a better person when you're in a predicament where the resources are scarce and your survival in left to the mercy of your keepers. Be your own man, son, and make the decisions you feel good about and not one that you will regret later because you didn't.

May 19, 2005 had arrived. I was scheduled to appear before the Board of Prison Terms for the eighth time. My hearing was set for 9:30 A.M. The attorney who was representing me was front and center when I was cleared to enter the chamber area. She pulled me in a private room and shared her plan before it was show time. All the players were in position and we all were on record. The hearing was conducted in typical fashion. The usual questions were asked, along with some thorough interrogating about my drug and alcohol use. Aside from that, how Lil Paul and I were managing was the next major area that was covered. They were surprised that he and I had been cellmates for over three years, and neither of us had gotten into any trouble. Recess for deliberation was announced at 11:50 A.M.

My attorney and I went to wait in the little boxed room. She needed to take a restroom break. So, I was left alone for a few moments. I said a prayer to God and poured my heart out asking for the Lord to touch those board members' hearts and give me favor. The attorney and I were able to have a discussion before the hearing resumed. She expressed how pleased she was by the way I conducted myself and believed that the outcome looked good for me.

We were back on record! All parties had returned to the room. The Panel was ready to proceed. The time was 12:45 P.M. This is the matter of Paul Scott, CDC number C-30580. Mr. Scott, the Panel has reviewed all information received from the public and relied on the following circumstances in concluding that you are not a danger to society or a threat to public safety. Therefore, you are found suitable for parole. I got a little emotional after hearing this.

But, for the most part, I kept myself together because I had been there before. The Presiding Commissioner continued on with the basis of their findings. He advised of the Decision Review Unit having 120 days to approve or deny these findings. And then the Governor's process.

At the conclusion, the Deputy Commissioner shared that what impressed her the most was the fact that my son and I, who I had never had a relationship with in society, were able to unite in a prison cell and manage a relationship for over three years without getting into any incidence. It was unheard of from a correctional perspective and defied all odds. From that, the ultimate evidence was present that you were ready for society, Mr. Scott. Good luck.

Chapter 16

Seek & You Shall Find

T he day was September 27, 2005. I received a notice to pick up legal mail from the office. It was only one thing that it could be, the Decision Review Unite. I went to the B-Quad office and got my legal mail right after dinner. Before opening it, I looked up into the sky and thanked the Lord for watching over me. I went and sat under a tree before opening and reading. Board of Prison Terms Decision Review Unit, September 24, 2005, was the date on it. That was also the day of my grandson's 8th birthday. The letter read, Mr. Scott, your parole consideration hearing was conducted on May 19, 2005. Decision Review is completed, and the final decision date of your hearing is September 15, 2005. The decision has been approved by the Board of Prison Terms. The Governor now had 30 days to exercise his review authority.

September 28, 2005, at 3:45 pm, the announcement was made over the institution paging system, Paul Scott, report to the control corridor. God had to be surely shining down on me because I was just leaving work, walking out the Protestant Chapel doors. As a matter of fact, I was walking past that exact area in which I was sitting that beautiful Saturday afternoon when I had the revelation while waiting for the Seventh-day Adventist community volunteers to come in. I continued walking. The B-Quad turnstile was situated at noon position from the Protestant Chapel. The entrance into the control corridor was situated at 1 o'clock in relation to the B-Quad turnstile. I proceeded to the control corridor.

During this time of the day, 3:45 pm, many inmates were returning to their housing sections from work assignments such as Industry, Laundry, Maintenance shops and Vocations. Everybody who was anybody knew that an inmate getting paged to report to the control corridor at 3:45 pm, 25 minutes before lock up for count time, could only be for one or two things. While I was walking toward the control corridor, I was greeted and acknowledged by several inmates who knew me and was aware of my situation. They extended their good lucks and positive energy in my direction.

I arrived in the control corridor. Before I could identify myself, the correctional officer on duty asked me if I was Paul Scott. My reply was yes, sir. He cleared me to go in the direction where it all happens, the hearings with the Board of Prison Terms. Once I got to the top of the stairs, another correctional officer was waiting for me. He asked for my inmate ID card and I produced it. He then instructed me to go inside this huge room designed just like the rooms the BPT hearings were conducted in. Upon my entering, I was addressed by another State of California employee. It was the Lifer Coordinator. "Good evening Mr. Scott." "Good evening, sir!" "Do you know why you were called down here today, Mr. Scott?" "Yes, I think it has something to do with the Board of Prison Terms finding me suitable for parole." "That is correct, Mr. Scott. Your case went before the Decision Review Unit and they approved the Panel's findings." "Yes, sir, I am aware of that. I received a notice through legal mail." "Good, the Governor now has an opportunity to review the Panel's decision and decide if he wants to confirm or reject their decision." "I understand that, sir, and that is what I am waiting to find out." "Well, Mr. Scott, the Governor, has declined to use his review authority in this matter. Do you know what that means?" "No sir, I don't, I have never made it this far." "Mr. Scott, it means you're going home." I thought all my tears were gone and that I would never cry again like I did over my mother's death. But, I am not too proud to say, that for a moment there I lost it and the flood gates were opened one more time. Only this time, these tears were of joy, victory, achievement, celebration, and love.

I was advised not to share the information I had just received with anyone I was not certain had my best interest at heart. There was a lot of tension building in the institution and portions of it were on lock down because of racial issues. So, it would be in my best interest to keep silent. The Lifer coordinator went on to advise me that I had a rule out, which meant I would be released once all documents were processed. My parole was a high risk, which meant my parole agent had to come pick me up. So, as soon as the parole agent could make plans to come get me was as soon as I could be released. I thanked the Lifer Coordinator and shook his and the correctional officer's hands as I exited the room.

Lil Paul was waiting for me at the gate as soon as I entered the Quad. He wanted to know what did I get paged to the control corridor for. I told him I would share it with him in the cell. As I keep walking, I was reminded that this was the same space I was in two years prior when Lil Paul had his skirmish and I was being propositioned to go to war. It was the same location Lil Paul and I packed our property and moved to another section which afforded us an opportunity to bond the best a father and son could under the circumstances and get free therapy, knowledge, and wisdom along the way. We were mocked and made fun of during our transition and now I had a chance to shine and return there behind my back insults that they thought I didn't know about. Yes, this was my opportunity to get even and let the crowds know who really was the ram in the bush. The different groups were out in their accustomed spots waiting for the word on what Paul Scott was paged to control corridor for.

I knew this thinking was immature and I had nothing left to prove. The people who I needed to impress were and I didn't want to jeopardize that. Some 10 minutes ago, I was sitting in front of a state employee who told me I was going home after 25 years in prison, and advised me to keep my business to myself. A man who goes home to his family every day and eat dinner with them at the table and watch television in his own living room. I think I better take his advice because he is already where I am trying to get. I did stop at one particular table of a group of inmates I knew would be terribly upset if I didn't update them on my status because they all were lifers and just word on somebody going home world restore hope in many. It had been a long time since a lifer was released from the California Men's Colony and over a decade since an Afro-American. "Hey brother Paul, what's good man? I heard them page for you to go upfront. What it look like for you." "Ah, man, it's all good! They were just letting me know that the full board review panel approved the findings and now I had to await the Governor's decision." "Okay, bro, hope things go well for you."

A page for Paul Scott to report to the control corridor was for me to be informed that my suitable for parole was approved by the full board panel was my story, and I stuck to it, at least for as long as I could. When Lil Paul and I were in the cell I let him know what was up! He was overwhelmed with joy and I had to calm him down.

I shared the plan of silence with him and how we would play the nonchalant role to throw people off. Lil Paul understood, agreed, and thought it was a good idea because he knew we were surrounded by jealousy and haters.

The next day, September 29, 2005, was a Thursday (September 29, 1980, was the date Lil Paul was conceived 25 years ago), I went to my work assignment just like nothing had ever happened. Thursday mornings from 8:30 am until 9:30 am was the time scheduled for Chapel workers meeting with the Rev. The meeting went as usual. Afterward, I had a private moment with the Rev. I informed the Rev. of my good news and the Rev. was very happy for me and stated over and over how I deserved it. I let the Rev. know to keep it completely confidential. The Rev. agreed! The rest of the day was great, and it was regular business. Although, Minister John Milton came in that afternoon to conduct some School of the Bible business since he was the Dean over it.

When the opportunity presented itself, I let Minister John Milton know about my blessing. He let out such a loud praise to God that it shook the Catholic Chapel walls next door. Both of Minister John Milton's legs were amputated. But I thought he was going to get out of his wheelchair and dance after I told him I was going home. I had only let one Chapel worker know prior to telling Minister John Milton because he was a lifer and was serious about his walk as a Christian. But everybody knew something was up after Minister John Milton finished rejoicing in the Lord and giving thanks.

The day ended and I was on my way back to B-Quad. When I entered the Quad, I was immediately approached by a real solider friend of mine named Big Clay. Big Clay worked in the Captain's office up front where any and all documentation for movement and activities were generated. "Big Paul, what's up, bro., I thought we were better than that?" "What you talking about, Big Clay?" Big Clay went in his upper left side shirt pocket and pulled out a ducat. A ducat was a pass for movement to different appointments, meetings, activities, and assignments. Some said priority and non-priority. Big Clay handed the ducat to me. It was a Priority Ducat for Scott, C-30580, to turn in ALL property at Receiving & Release for Parole Processing at 8:30 am on 9/30/2005. What could I say! Big Clay and I embraced right there on the spot and he congratulated me. I thanked him for looking out for me because had he given the ducat to my cell floor officer, everybody in the building would have none my business. Big Clay understood and said he probably would have done the same thing after being locked up for 25 years. We went and purchased some sodas and walked the yard.

All the inmates were hanging out and they knew something was up for Big Clay and Big Paul to both be walking the yard together just out of the clear blue. No, it was more to the picture and inmates who didn't have any business of their own of importance were always in prisoner(s) business who were trying to better themselves. Big Clay had been incarcerated for about 21 years at this time. He just wanted to know what it felt like to realize that I was going home after 25 years. I told Big Clay that I couldn't give him anyone answer. But that I was feeling a number of different emotions. I did go on to say that if I were to make a selection as to which emotion I was experiencing the most, it would in no doubt be fear. Big Clay looked at me and said," what!" I said, "man, I am going into a world that is completely new to me and I am scared. The main thing I had working for me was a large support system of family and friends who wanted to see me win. On that note, it was yard recall.

During count time, I showed the ducat to Lil Paul. He was blown away! "Pops, you going home for real," was what he exclaimed! I couldn't even respond. I just stood up looking out the window and thinking about all the years I wondered if I would ever drive an automobile again. Lil Paul and I talked about the things he wanted me to do for Jeremiah. I promised him that it would be done. I started getting the items packed that I needed to turn in at Receiving & Release the following day.

I made a phone call home that same evening. I called my niece Sonya which is whose home I was scheduled to parole. Before I could even share the news of my being cleared to come home, she was telling me about the parole agent came by her home to make sure everything was in compliance for me to live there. She started crying and said the man said you are coming home, Uncle Paul, that they are finally going to let you come home. I told her yes, and that was the reason for my call. Then she let me know that the parole agent was coming to get me on Monday, October 3, 2005 and that she and other family members would be there waiting to welcome me.

The next morning arrived. I had four boxes of property all to be mailed home. Lil Paul went and got the cart for me to put them on and roll out the building. We packed the boxes on the carted and headed out the building. I had an old baseball hat I was wearing trying to look incognito. As we exited the building and hit the track, Lil Paul was strolling by my side as I was pushing the cart. We got in front of the benches in front of building three and the card table on the other side of the track next to the baseball diamond. Big Ernie from Compton said, "Hey, Big Paul, where you going with all your property, bro?" "Hah Big Ernie, I'm going out to court on a custody matter." Big Ernie said, "BS, you ain't going out to court, you going home!" Big Ernie and another brother came and grabbed the cart I was pushing and said they got this. This took place right before work call. It seemed like the whole yard went up in celebration following Big Ernie's words. When we got to the gate, the correctional officer had to open the gate for me to get out with the cart. I pulled the priority ducat out and the coast was cleared. All I could think of as I pushed the cart the remainder of the way to Receiving & Release, "vengeance is mine: I will repay, saith the Lord."

Minister John Milton delivered the message for the Sunday morning service. At the conclusion, many stayed back and the Rev. allowed us to have a little spread. In the process of us all sitting around eating, fellowshipping and giving testimonies, different brothers shared what my contribution to their relationship with

Christ meant. We had a group prayer and Minister John Milton said a prayer over me as I was prepared to parole the next day.

Sunday night service, Pastor Bonds had me come up and share what God had placed on my heart. That evening, it was not enough space to contain all the inmates who attended the service on the evening of October 2, 2005. The doors had to be closed and it all was to and for the glory of God. There were prisoners in the congregation that I had served time with for more years than I could remember some of them I had never seen at a church service who were there that night. The word had spread that I was going home and they wanted to rub off on them what God had blessed me with. Pastor Bond had me pray over everyone who came to the altar that night. The service got real emotional and Pastor Bonds just allowed everybody who wanted to stay back and fellowship to do so at the end of the service. Pastor Bonds prayed over me and said he would see me in the morning and watch God's work walk out those gates.

Lil Paul and I stayed up as long as we could talking. We fell asleep with the light and television on. I had been sitting in the chair. Once I realized what time it was, I put my bunk down and dozed off to sleep but wasn't able to fall into a deep sleep. Daybreak came and it was showtime. I showed up and got prepared. I was wearing a sweat suit that my mother had sent me in a package in 1997. I had never worn it before and always said the day I get released; it was what I would wear in memory and honor of my mother.

Lil Paul walked to Receiving & Release with me and waited as I was getting processed. The Captain's Office was right across from R & R. Big Clay came over and kicked things around with Lil Paul and I while the process was taking place. A Doctor who I saw for several years for my hypertension even came down to wish me success, stated she knew I would do well and advised me to contact her when I discharged my parole. The Receiving & Released Sergeant informed me that my parole agent was on site and to say my goodbyes.

Lil Paul walked with me as far as he could go, which was in the control corridor. We embraced and said our, "will see you at home!" I had already made arrangement for Stan Johnson to move in the cell with Lil Paul when I left. He was a good brother that I could trust with my life. Stan had been incarcerated for 28 years and did his own time. In fact, Stan was the brother who told me to give him 50 pushups that time I was tripping about the toothpicks. Pastor Bonds kept his word and was waiting for me in the parking lot and greeted me with an embrace as he welcomed me to the free world.

Chapter 17

Nobody asked Me...Words from Lil Paul

I am not big on talking. I like to keep my thoughts and feelings to myself and act on them rather than talk about them. Maybe this is because when I was a kid, nobody asked me how I felt or what I was thinking. If they did, I didn't hear them. For whatever the reason may have been, I didn't hear them. And that is what leads to the next misconception; it was assumed that I was okay with the way everything was, but nobody asked me, and I never had a chance to voice who I was because I didn't know, and nobody asked me.

I knew who my father was from two different perspectives; the one when I visited him in prison; and the one from the image that he left on the streets. I became more acquainted with the one on the streets than I did with the one I visited in prison because I was around that image more often. At some point in my childhood development, I thought it was expected of me to be like my dad. Nobody told me otherwise, and from the image of him that was being presented to me from most of the people who knew him, how could it have been any different.

In the bible, Ecclesiastes 3:1 says, there is a time for everything, and a season for every activity under the Heavens. Well, maybe, just maybe, my going to prison and sharing a prison cell with my father for four years was God's way of letting me get to know my Pops for myself. I was able to see him with my own eyes and make my own opinion about him. My father may have went to prison for doing bad things and breaking the law. But he wasn't doing bad things and breaking the law anymore, which is what I thought he was doing and that that was the reason they wouldn't let him come home. But that wasn't true and I had to ask for forgiveness. If the truth really be told, my Pops was helping run the place and he was doing more work for God in prison than most people do with their ministries in society and getting results.

Now, I will be honest and tell on myself right here. There were times that I got really upset when I would see my dad given all his time and attention to caring for the mentally ill prisoners and his involvement in the ministry. I understood that it was his job and calling. But it began to take away from the relationship we were building. I had never lived with my dad, so this was an important time. And he would always tell me to value every minute in the day because if you lost a second, you couldn't get it back. I would also get angry with the administration because, at times, they treated my dad as if they owned him and to an extent, I guess it was true. They can make you work for free; they tell you what you can and cannot do, and most if not all your rights were taken away as a citizen of the United States of America.

There were many things that I learned about myself and life that I probably never would have had I not went to prison and got to know, my dad. I am not saying I'm glad I went to prison. But I am saying I'm glad it was with my dad. I was angry with him at first and I blamed him for a lot of things that happened in my life. There were many things that I was never asked and because of that I learned to suppress and hide my feelings like my being angry at my dad because I felt like he abandoned me. Abandonment can be looked at in different ways. For example, when I was a kid and would go and visit my dad and the time came for us to leave, I felt abandoned then. And I felt that each and every time. Nobody asked me about that. I liked going to visit my dad, but I didn't like it when I had to leave. When I would be talking to my dad on the phone and time came for the call to end, I didn't understand that, and it would cause that feeling of abandonment to come up for me to feel one more time.

So, when I say, "Nobody Asked Me," what I mean is nobody asked me the different ways I felt abandoned. As I got older, when things would happen that reminded me of abandonment experiences I had, I would feel that pain I was holding inside all over again. People get made fun of and placed in all kinds of stereotype categories and looked at as sensitive when they start addressing issues in life that deal with: Rejection, Overlooked, Disregarded, Not Noticed, Deserted, Disrespected and Offended. And I believe that is the reason many people stay like they are because of fear and being made fun of. We find ways to cover it up instead of confronting it.

I share this from my own experience. The blessing was in my father, and I having a chance to build the relationship that we never had and making the best of it was the miracle. My dad don't get caught all up in trying to impress people by bragging or boasting. And if he does, he do it where God gets the glory. But the point I would like to make here is that I may have thought my dad abandoned me in society. But when I came to prison, he stepped up and fully fulfilled his role as my father. He got me sent to the prison he was at and we stayed together for four years and four months until he got released first. My dad made sure we were not separated and stood on God's word that says: No weapon formed against thee shall prosper and every tongue that shall rise against thee in judgment thou shall condemn. My dad is my hero because he prevailed over every trap that was set to destroy him and then took me under his wing and navigated our terrain to freedom.

My father has been home now for close to 15 years, and I have been home for 13 years. We both are living successful lives doing God's work and helping make a difference in the Lives of 'The Least of God's People!' To God be the Glory.

Message from the Author

A Child feeling abandoned by his/her parent can result in any number of different ways. Consequently, it can cause various antisocial behaviors to develop and impede their overall maturity as a person. Lil Paul became united with his father in a prison cell after being conceived 21 years prior to their endeavor. They never lived together in society because two days following Lil Paul's conception, his father was arrested and never released until October 3, 2005.

Abandonment is a huge issue; many human beings walk around effected by the damage without ever realizing it and/or seeking any help. Paul Scott hopes after you finish reading this book, that you have a better understanding of the subtle forms of abandonment as well as betrayal. Furthermore, he trusts that you have a deep burning desire to work on enriching your relationships with your sons, daughters, mothers, and fathers if you were able to relate with any of the information contained in this book

It is the author's prayer that this book assists you, the reader, in confronting and healing from any injuries you may have suffered as a result of feeling rejected in any form or capacity.

About the Author

Paul Scott Sr. is a father, grandfather, Ordained Elder, American Chaplain, Grief Counselor Specialist, Substance Abuse Counselor, Credible Messenger, and Healthy Living Enthusiast. He currently resides in the state of Georgia but travels where needed and appropriately requested to utilize his skills to help correct and heal the wrongs, the damage, hurts, and pains of life. It is his prayer after you finish reading this book; you have a deep burning desire to work on enriching your relationship with your son, daughter, mother, or father. Furthermore, for your awareness to recognize the subtly forms of abandonment, rejection, and betrayal expands, and you feel encouraged to address the issues that are needed in your life or someone you care about. I hope your healing has begun, and if not, that it begins today.

Direct all inquiries and correspondence to/

Heads Up Publications
*c/o Paul Scott Sr. **OR** Paul Scott Jr.*
P.O Box 162593
Atlanta, GA 30321

Made in the USA
Columbia, SC
04 June 2020

98440532R00107